DELEUZE: A G
THE PERP.

Also available from Continuum:

DELEUZE: A GUIDE FOR THE PERPLEXED

CLAIRE COLEBROOK

continuum
LONDON • NEW YORK

CONTINUUM
The Tower Building
11 York Road
London SE1 7NX

15 East 26th Street
New York
NY 10010

First published 2006
www.continuumbooks.com

British Library Cataloguing-in-Publication Data
A catalogue record for this book is available from the British Library.

ISBN: HB: 0 8264 78298
PB: 0 8264 78301

Library of Congress Cataloging-in-Publication Data
Colebrook, Claire.
    Deleuze : a guide for the perplexed / Claire Colebrook.
    p.   cm.
    Includes bibliographical references and index.
    ISBN 0-8264-7829-8 (hardback) – ISBN 0-8264-7830-1 (pbk.)
    1. Deleuze, Gilles.   I. Title.
    B2430.D454C64 2006
    194–dc22

2005023356

Typeset by Servis Filmsetting Ltd, Manchester
Printed and bound in Great Britain by MPG Books Ltd, Cornwall

CONTENTS

To Rosi Braidoth and Anneke Smelik,
whose hospitality, kindness and library
made the completion of this book possible

ABBREVIATIONS

Works by Gilles Deleuze

B	*Bergsonism* (1988)
C1	*Cinema 1: The Movement-Image* (1986)
C2	*Cinema 2: The Time-Image* (1989)
CC	*Essays Critical and Clinical* (1997)
DR	*Difference and Repetition* (1994)
ES	*Empiricism and Subjectivity: An Essay on Hume's Theory of Human Nature* (1991)
F	*Foucault* (1988)
KCP	*Kant's Critical Philosophy* (1984)
LB	*The Fold: Leibniz and the Baroque* (1993)
LS	*The Logic of Sense* (1990)
N	*Nietzsche and Philosophy* (1983)
PS	*Proust and Signs* (2000)
S	*Expressionism in Philosophy: Spinoza* (1990)

Works by Gilles Deleuze and Félix Guattari

AO	*Anti-Oedipus* (1977)
K	*Kafka: Toward a Minor Literature* (1986)
TP	*A Thousand Plateaus* (1987)
WP	*What is Philosophy?* (1994)

INTRODUCTION

This book is a general account and defence of the *philosophy* of Gilles Deleuze. It begins, however, with a lengthy discussion of Deleuze's books on cinema. Far from being an 'example' of Deleuze's thought, his engagement with cinema, and the fact that his philosophy takes the form of such an engagement, is essential to the very nature of his philosophy. If there is one idea that has domesticated Deleuze's thought it is the idea that Deleuze is a vitalist.[1] Whereas other French poststructuralist thinkers focused intensely on the ways in which life, presence, being or the real were constituted through systems (such as language), Deleuze always explained the genesis of systems from life. It has been possible, then, to attribute a mysticism to Deleuze, such that he affirms some ultimate vital life that we can intuit only in the living forms it creates, never as it is in itself (for on such a model there could be no life in itself, only life's creations). There is a partial truth in this idea, for the concept of life, and the commitment to forming a concept of life, is crucial to Deleuze's philosophy. But the concept of life that Deleuze spends his entire philosophical life creating is the concept of *difference*: it is possible to intuit life as difference – not life as some thing that then changes and differs, but life as the power *to differ*. If, as Deleuze argues, philosophy is the active creation of concepts and *not* the acceptance of already formed images of what counts as good or commonsensical thinking, then *the* philosophical concept *par excellence* would be the concept of difference. Deleuze therefore rejects the idea that philosophy is pure or purely formal; philosophy is not the tidying up of errors, nor is it the creation of a logic abstracted from everyday thinking, nor a reduction to what must be required by any truthful, rational subject. On the contrary, *thinking* is at once an activity of life, but

1

a life that does not inevitably or necessarily think. All around us, despite the claims of philosophy and rationalism, we encounter the absence of thinking, the malevolence and stupidity that go well beyond error. So if thinking is *not* necessary, but only a potential, we need to ask two questions: What is life such that thinking became possible? How did something like the *thought* of life emerge?

Deleuze does not assume that there is life as some evolving, striving, developing power that creates a human brain that can then understand that originating life. He confronts the possibility that thought might *not* have emerged – the tendency towards the absence of thinking. In *Anti-Oedipus* he will, with Félix Guattari, argue that it is *desire* that we should consider first, with life *and* death being ways in which desire produces both organisms and their dissolution. This means that instead of opposing a creative flowing life to a negative and destructive death, Deleuze and Guattari posit *one* plane or substance – desire – from which life and death emerge. On the one hand, they argue, there is the life of the *organism*: the life of a human body that has a certain stable continuity and then dies. Too often Western thinking has defined life from this image of a living body. Opposed to this is Deleuze and Guattari's concept of desire; desire is both life and death, for at a quite literal level, the death of this or that body is not at all negative. Without the death of organisms there would be no change, evolution or life in its radical sense. This radical sense of life – the life that is not that of the bounded organism with its *own* life – is what Deleuze and Guattari refer to as the 'body without organs'. The body without organs, in *Anti-Oedipus*, is that which is other than the closed organism:

> The body without organs is the model of death . . . The death model appears when the body without organs repels the organs and lays them aside: no mouth, no tongue, no teeth – to the point of self-mutilation, to the point of suicide. Yet there is no real opposition between the body without organs and the organs as partial objects; the only real opposition is to the molar organism that is their common enemy . . . Hence it is absurd to speak of a death desire that would presumably be in qualitative opposition to the life desires. Death is not desired, there is only death that desires, by virtue of the body without organs or the immobile motor, and there is also life that desires, by virtue of the working organs.[2]

It is not, then, that we have self-furthering, fecund, flowing, world-disclosing life on the one hand and the punctual, inert, isolated corpse on the other. For what we need to understand, Deleuze and Guattari argue, is that it is the *organism* that opposes the principle of life and death, and that the image of the organism is really opposed to *desire*. Not an opposition between flowing life and inert death, but a relation between the bounded organism and desire. Not, then, an ethics of maximizing life, of re-living flow, genesis and production in opposition to the non-relational or inert. Instead a thought of the desire which is *both* life (as multiple degrees of difference) and death as zero intensity, where we can imagine any life form – such as thinking – being reduced to zero, and we can also think of many points in life when this zero degree is approached (in cases of torture, bodily exhaustion or cultural inanity). In addition to the clear and everyday world of positive things there is also the necessary world of zero intensities, for we could not imagine any quality unless there were the possibility of its zero intensity, the point where it would no longer make a difference or be felt:

> The experience of death is the most common of occurrences in the unconscious, precisely because it occurs in life and for life, in every passage or becoming, in every intensity as passage or becoming. It is in the very nature of every intensity to invest within itself the zero intensity starting from which it is produced.[3]

Well before composing *Anti-Oedipus* with Guattari, Deleuze had given strict philosophical reasons for rejecting the idea of life as some ultimate foundation from which mind, bodies and language would flow – a life that would be opposed to a death of non-creation, inertia and indifference. Deleuze was insistent that 'life' in its more radical sense would already include what we normally take to be death. Deleuze refuses to see deviations, redundancies, destructions, cruelties or contingency as accidents that befall or lie outside life; life and death were aspects of desire or 'the plane of immanence'. This presents us with *the* challenge of Deleuze's philosophy. All traditional philosophy – all unthinking morality – begins within an opposition between life and death: the good is what furthers life, while evil is the destruction of life. Evil is opposed to or outside life. We could say, for example, that art is corrupt because it is a mere copy of life, only an image or distortion. Or we could say that art enlivens life, helping us to feel the power of our own creative spirit. Deleuze, however, does not rely on any such pre-established opposition. Instead of saying that something is good because it furthers life he asks the much more difficult question of just *what style* of life something – a political form, a work of art or a philosophy – enables. Deleuze's concept of life is therefore not vitalist, and for two reasons. First, although he considers it responsible to question how any activity or event emerged – so that we should not begin from rational 'man' but ask about how he is possible and what the life is that he expresses – he also studies genesis and emergence in terms of potentiality rather than actuality. That is, we should not begin from the rational individual and ask what life must be such that reason is possible; we should see rationality as *one* way in which a much broader potential is expressed. This means that life is not reducible to what has actually been produced,[4] to the world as it has unfolded; for life, when thought properly, is a power or potential to create (and *not* the creation *of* some proper or destined end).[5] Second, Deleuze demonstrates that life can only be thought adequately, and that we only release the full potential of thinking, when thought encounters what is *not* itself. Philosophy can only begin to think when it steps outside its own images of mind, reason and humanity.[6] This is why Deleuze installs technology at the heart of philosophy *and* life. Human life *does* have a power or potential to think, but we can only understand this power, not when life unfolds from itself, but when this power encounters other powers. Only when the human brain confronts what is not itself can it be pushed to the maximum; only in confronting the *unthought*, the *accidental* and the *unthinking* do we begin to think. Only when the human encounters the inhuman will we know what the human body can do, and only when life opens itself up to violence, destruction, death and zero intensity will we be able to discern just what counts as 'a' single life – its precarious distance and emergence from all its potentials *not* to be. For this reason the first part of this book will be concerned with Deleuze's work on cinema, for it was here that he showed how creative philosophy and the human brain might become if we confronted our relation to machines.

On the traditional understanding, technology is added on to life. First there is life in its striving, self-expansion and growth and then technology *extends* life's own power. We can then condemn technology when it no longer serves life but enslaves it. We imagine that there are living powers to think, remember and imagine, and *then* technological devices, such as writing, recording and symbolism, which render the living form more regular, systematic and stable. On such an understanding we would consider life as it is actually given – thinking human life – and then consider technology as an extension. This idea of technology as a supplement or as not *really* living yields a limited understanding of the virtual. The images, creations and reproductions of life are regarded as secondary, or added on to life; so that 'virtual reality' is regarded as a mere add-on. Now Deleuze makes two key manoeuvres in subverting the relation between life and image, and this comes out most clearly in his work on cinema but is also evident early in his work with his definition of overturning Platonism.

First, Deleuze redefines the simulacrum, not as a secondary image of life, but as life itself.[7] That is, there is not a full and present life, sufficient unto itself and fully actualized, which *then* relates to what is not itself by forming images or representations. So Deleuze does not begin from a mind or consciousness that must somehow come to know or find its outside world; he does not begin philosophy from the question of 'what can we know?' or 'how accurate are the images we have of the world?' He does not begin from human life or the life of the organism and then ask how consciousness came into being, for he does not regard life as a set of things or organisms that *then* perceives. Rather, life is perception, or a virtual power *to relate* and *to image*.[8] There could not be mind or consciousness, for example, without the connection between the brain, the body, the body's organs and external stimuli. These connections among the bodily parts that form both the human organism, and the human organism's relation to the world, are perceptions or images. Evolving life is nothing more than a web of perceptive responses – cells responding and adapting to other cells to form simple life forms, those life forms responding to or 'perceiving' environments. There is not a mind or life and *then* the perception of images, for life *is imaging*, a plane of relations that take the form of 'perceptions' precisely because something '*is*' only its responses. Before there are actual terms – 'mind' on the one hand, 'world' on the other – there is a potential for relation, and relations for Deleuze are best described as 'images'.

Deleuze does not regard human consciousness or mind as the sole point of image and relation; he is certainly not arguing that the world is constituted by a consciousness that synthesizes appearances into some meaningful whole. For there are images, simulations or perceptions before and beyond consciousness. A cell's life is actualized by the connections it makes with other cells; each cell would have the potential for a multiplicity of relations, but in this world it is actualized in this relation (but there could be other relations, other possible worlds). The wasp, in order to live and be a wasp, must connect with an orchid, and the orchid can maintain its life only with the wasp's migration from orchid to orchid. Life, then, is not a being that *then* evolves or differs, but is the potential to differ, a potential that is actualized in connections and relations among powers. Why refer to these relations, connections and production as a process of simulation or 'imaging'? The key point is that for Deleuze a power or potential does not have its relations determined in advance, so while waves of light *might* be perceived as colour by the eye, one could imagine another world in which the potential for colour might be actualized differently; light waves could be perceived as heat. And while the eye itself evolved as a response to the problem of light there could also have been other lines of creation.

By describing relations as perceptions or images, Deleuze draws upon and extends Henri Bergson's idea of pure perception. One can imagine a limit case of 'pure perception', where one term relates to another immediately and completely – an eye, for example, that would absorb all the rays of light and fluctuations fully and completely. (This would have to be a God's-eye view, for every actual eye has to adopt a point of view and perceives light in its own way.) One could imagine molecular life as having something close to such an unmediated perception; one molecule does not decide or imagine its relation to another. But insofar as each molecule responds to its outside and encounters, it is perceptive. A hydrogen atom behaves in a certain way – or *is* – when it connects with oxygen, and these connections in turn behave or perceive according to their connections. We could refer to this as 'molecular perception' insofar as the relation produced is determined by the way each term's potential is realized in specific relation to another power or potential. Ideally, 'pure perception' would be a relation without delay. Human perception, by contrast, perceives what is other than itself in its own terms, the eye reducing the complexity of fluctuations and differences to a world of stable objects. Human perception exists in a 'zone of indetermination', such that the power of the eye to see might be realized either by a contemplative affection – where the image is received but not acted on – or by action – where the image prompts the sensory-motor apparatus of the human body to move and act. Human perception might therefore be located at a midway point between a molecular perception that is nothing other than what it receives, with no delay or decision – a pure act – and a pure perception that in not acting, moving or selecting from received images is capable of perceiving the difference and multiple potential of what is presented (a God's-eye view or grasp of the whole of life).[9] But such a pure perception is only a limit; in life there is always a selection and asymmetry from one power to another. Deleuze does, however, work with these two limits in all his philosophy, imagining both 'zero intensity' when a perception makes *no* difference or relation, and philosophy which is the potential for 'infinite speed', or the thought of a potential in all its possible relations. Philosophy is the power of the brain to delay an *active* relation to images, where we select and move according to the needs of life, in order to achieve a pure contemplative relation, allowing the images in all their complexity, difference and potential to be thought.

Thinking, then, would be the maximization not of living matter but of the virtual; instead of acting upon the differences that confront us for the sake of the specific actualized organism that we are, we might think of those images and differences for themselves, as they would be for any being whatever, beyond the human and its specific organizing interests. All life is simulation; there is no proper image. Any actualization of a power is only a specific limitation of that power's potential. The world we see is one possible world, one expression or actualization of a world of powers and potentials that hold other worlds, or 'lines of flight'; these lines can be released *not* by intensifying who we already are and realizing our humanity, but by creating new relations, new actualizations of the potentials that have, up until now, produced the 'man' of good sense, common sense and Western reason.[10]

This leads to the second key intervention of Deleuze's work. If we can only realize the virtual potential of imaging life by releasing ourselves from the human point of view, then technology will not be an *extension* of human life, a way of humanity mastering and maximizing its own power. Technology will allow for new connections and intersections – new perceptions. It is in this sense that cinema, for Deleuze, does not only demand a new philosophy, or a new consideration of what it is to think. Cinema is a technology that will release the human from what it *actually is* and allow it to imagine itself, and its world, differently, to release its inhuman[11] potential. For this reason, also, the first chapter of this book will begin by looking at Deleuze's work on cinema. There has been a tendency to read Deleuze as a vitalist and a neo-Platonist, or as a thinker primarily motivated by mathematics and physics,[12] as if all his writings on cinema, literature, painting, science and politics[13] were merely *instances* of expressive life, a life that ultimately remained original, in-itself and the cause of all becoming. On such a reading no actual being would be adequate to the thought of life, and so philosophy would strive to overcome the expressions of life to arrive at an intuition of expressive difference itself. But such a reading of Deleuze must discount the emphasis Deleuze placed on the expressions or actualizations of life that create a new whole of life. The idea of the 'open whole', so crucial to his work on cinema, refers to a life that does not exist outside of its expressions; there is not a life that *then* unfolds in time in different beings. Rather, the unfolding of time is the *undoing* of being, the proliferation of difference, and the destruction of any closed form. Cinema, or the creation of the connection among images, and the coupling of the human eye with those images, demonstrates that a particular and contingent connection – the camera and the eye – can open a new thought of how it is that life connects. This in turn will open a new life, new potentials. That is, the creations of philosophy, science and art do not passively *read* life; they re-create life. If we think differently about time today because of the advent of cinema, then this does not just mean that we have a different idea or image of life; it means that life itself is different (and that we realize that 'life itself' is just this potential to be different). Although, then, the following two chapters focus on cinema, they do so only insofar as cinema is a new beginning. Once we realize what cinema has made possible, how it helps us to think differently, then we will also be able to approach politics, art and philosophy differently.

CHAPTER 1

CINEMA, THOUGHT AND TIME

DELEUZE'S CINEMA BOOKS

Deleuze's two cinema books (published in French in 1983 and 1985 and translated into English in 1986 and 1987) are, obviously, books about cinema – the first having to do with classical cinema, or cinema up until the Second World War and the works of Orson Welles, the second concerned with modern cinema dominated by Resnais, Bresson and Godard. More importantly, however, these books are dominated by an argument concerning time and space. This argument extends beyond the subject of cinema and is inter-twined with an audacious claim regarding the very nature of life. It is no accident, and certainly not for reasons of metaphor, that Deleuze throughout his work refers to 'machines' of life, for his entire corpus is dominated by the concept of a life that *is* 'machinic': a proliferation of connections among natural *and* technical powers. The eye that encounters the cinematic screen forms a machine, but so does the hand that encounters the earth and acts as a tool; the flows of genetic material that make up any life-form are machines precisely because the forms they compose can reconfigure and reconnect to produce other forms. We could even argue, as Deleuze does, that 'the brain is a screen', as it is made up of the encounters that it takes up and which it organizes through the body's active and passive powers.[1] The history of cinema is not an event *within* human history, for 'humanity' is transformed through the machines it produces and encounters; 'man' becomes a quite different machine when he couples with the cinematic apparatus. In addition to making a claim regarding life as that which alters through its pro-ductions, differing with each invention, Deleuze also suggests that a series of changes – such as human technological history – might also make a qualititative or distinct leap, such that one machine might be capable of opening up a radically different style of production. Cinema may well be just this sort of machine (but it may also be the literary or architectural machines that really transform life; Deleuze and Guattari remain open to the potentials of a number of technologies and it remains to be seen just how their legacy will be extended[2]). Cinema, Deleuze insists, is not just one more technology or practice that allows us to manage life in new and interesting ways, and it is not just a cultural practice that might revolutionize life (although it may well be revolutionary in ways that are remarkably important). Rather, cinema is a technology that allows 'us' – humans possessed of a brain that bears an entire history of thought – to rethink our relation to technology, recognizing that our history is itself technological, a history made up of reconfiguring, mutating and proliferating machines. Cinema is the encounter between the machine of the brain-eye-body and the machine of the camera-screen. And it is this encounter that opens thought to the history of the human, and, if pushed further, allows thought to transcend the human. The cinematic technology that apparently supplements and constitutes the human opens on to the inhuman.

TECHNOLOGY

Before we see how this passage to the inhuman through technology is imagined by Deleuze we need to make a few cautionary definitions. First, technology needs to be understood in its essential sense – and this will take us directly to the broader arguments regarding space and time. Technology (from the Greek *techne*) is any repeatable or regular practice that maximizes the efficiency of life.[3] To a certain extent (and we will come back to this throughout this book) *seeing* is a technology: perception does not grasp or take in everything that is there to be seen by the eye.[4] Rather, we tend to perceive the world in ways already mastered by the eye, recognizing this scene as similar to so many others, populated by so many recognizable conceptualized objects. The technology of vision, like all technologies, is not life itself, nor is it a pure perception that fully comprehends the complexity and difference to which it is exposed. A technology is both an extension of life's potential – so that writing is an extension of the brain – and a transformation of life, for once we can write we can create sciences and philosophies that open up new potentials. A technology is there-fore both a continuation of life *and* a loss of life, for without forgoing some paths and actualizing some potentials rather than others, life would not be able to go on living. In this sense, then, the question of technology, when considered from a Deleuzian point of view, requires a redefinition of life: life is nothing more than a potential for expres-sions, productions and movements, but such expressions are contin-gent – some paths will be actualized, others will not. There is, then, a necessary non-production or non-actualization (a 'remaining-virtual') in the ongoing actualization of life.

A technology is an already established set of relations allowing for ongoing maximization of energy, but any saving of energy for the sake of life has to renounce *some* life. The eye cannot take in and interro-gate every fluctuation in its visual field; its grasp of basic objects allows it to make its way in the world efficiently, organized as it is in the set of relations that make up the moving human body. As the eye and embodied brain go through history, technologies ranging from language through to spectacles, telescopes, microscopes, cameras and computers allow human movements to be undertaken with less thought and energy, thereby allowing for the creation of further tech-nologies.[5] This already means that history is not a sequence where a body – the human body – passes through time, but is already a plane of varying speeds. Technologies that allow the eye to take less time – such as concepts that allow us to see a scene and grasp its sense almost immediately – require more effort and labour at the level of script and voice. One can imagine the eye of an infant struggling to take in and master the scene around it, moving slowly through its world. As the child gains the technologies of visual forms, concepts, language and the motor efficiency of its body, it can make more movements more quickly. With a sophisticated enough understanding the brain can grasp what is *not* even visually present. Sense, or the capacity to think what would be true beyond the present, is thought moving at 'infinite speed'. It is possible to read the current point of human history *either* as a mastery of technology moving at lightning speed, such that the human is overleaping itself, so empowered that it is never the same or at rest; *or* as an encroaching senility – we have become so accustomed to what is outside that we have stopped thinking, stopped *experien-cing*. Deleuze suggests that we are poised between these two possibil-ities: a life that can speed up its rate of change in order to become radically different *and* a life so habituated to its styles of change that it ceases to become, ceases to live. Both these possibilities are possibilities of capitalism, which according to Deleuze and Guattari is both a radical *deterritorialization*, such that all movements, parts and connections can be varied to allow for change, and a *reterritorialization* such that all such change is related to the one axiom of money. The aim of Deleuze's philosophy is, then, to free the positive potential of capitalism – the capacity for life to create ever-new connections and potentials – from its regressive or archaic tendencies to reduce those connections to one axiomatic of production. Technology is crucial to this problem, because technology is evidence both of life's radical expressive power and of the tendency to fall into rigid systems.

Cinema's status as a technology in history is exemplary. The cinematic distribution, multiplication and reproduction of images have allowed us to see more while perceiving less: we 'know' New York, the Renaissance, America in the 1950s, and even the prehistoric fictional worlds of *Jurassic Park*, and all this without the labour of perception. Cinema has contributed to a certain ready-madeness of the world. And this is why its first anti-technology detractors (including Deleuze's much-loved Henri Bergson) concluded that cinema intensified a laziness of human life and thinking: we tend to see the world in simplified, static and habitual terms; we cut reality into snapshots or pre-formed static wholes.[6] Cinema according to Bergson exemplifies and intensifies a tendency for human life to fail to live; the technologies formed to master life and propel movement forward become rigid and reduce the creative potentials of life from which they have emerged. Even worse, the mind tends to see itself in the fixed terms it needed to apply to the material object world; we imagine the mind as a camera, a thing taking pictures of a world, rather than as a living, changing, creative and open power. In subjecting ourselves to technologies, such as cinema, the ease we have created precludes us from ever taking the full time to see and live the world as it really is. The technology that enhances life, allowing it to be more creative, can become so habitual that it masters life, becoming rigid, stagnant and inhuman. Cinema can exacerbate the tendency to cliché, stereotype and plot, where the future is reduced to already experienced forms, and time can pass only as the repetition of the same – a series of sequels where the brain becomes lulled into an easy and inactive consumption.[7] Time certainly seems to move forward when we watch *Star Wars 1*, *Star Wars 2*, *Star Wars 3* and so on. But that is just the problem. Time 'moves forward' – appears as a spatial series – because what the brain encounters is a sequence of equivalent and comparable things that can be laid out beside each other precisely because they are roughly equal. What is seen, what is other than the brain, remains the same, allowing the brain to consume each object as similar in a continuous series, building up a line of time. If, however, the forms presented were a 'shock to thought', the brain would have to reinvent itself, struggle to come to terms with the images. Instead of films or images being presented in an orderly sequence that confirms expectation and allows for a viewer *who goes through time* (what Deleuze refers to as the chronological time of *Chronos*), the viewer would be re-created and time would be divergent (time as the power of change or *Aion*).

Deleuze radicalizes Bergson and all those modernist thinkers who regarded technology as a fall into lifelessness and mechanization. Cinema bears the potential to free thought and perception from technology *through technology*; the very machines that extend life allowing for the reduction of effort can also open up new problems and new creations. This potential for overcoming technology resides in the fact that the human, in its everyday form, *is* a technology – a set of regular, repeatable and relatively unthinking habits. We become human by mastering life, which also means that something like the 'human' must be organized into a relatively stable form that is differentiated from its outside. We could, following Deleuze and Guattari, call this 'territorialization' and note that the very beginning of thought requires some reduction of the complex differences of life into *at least* two terms or points, such as eye and object, or mouth and food, or bodily surface and warmth. There is an initial orientation or 'map', which gains in complexity until, perhaps, there are ideas or concepts that can go beyond the body's movements and have movements of *sense*. Every animal, for example, has a map of its world – what it can and cannot eat, what is and is not to be feared – and every animal is also a territory, for it can live only by connecting with an environment and other bodies in its environment. The human animal, in addition to these spatial maps and territories can also create virtual maps – so that we can, for example, create concepts. We can think and make connections among absent or non-spatial objects, such as numbers, ideas or qualities. By reducing life's complexity and chaos to fixed terms that suit 'us' we produce the world and humanity as relatively stable moving wholes. The human is just this style of efficiency: a development of language, conceptuality, arithmetic, geometry, physics and history that allows us to live each present *without* inventing ourselves anew. We come into the world, as human, because each 'now' in all its complexity and newness has already been mastered and can therefore be treated as pretty much the same as any other. Technologies have retained the past into the future by rendering action and thoughts repeatable, allowing us to short-circuit invention and innovation.

ESSENCES

While cinema could, then, be seen as one more instance of technology that masters and homogenizes the world, its essence is far more radical. If technology is the repeatable, the regular, or the habituated practice that maximizes efficiency by maintaining relative stability through time – thereby rendering time relatively homogeneous, with each moment much like every other (such that we can consider all time as the time *of* one being, 'man') – *essences* are at the other end of Deleuze's thought of life. It is customary to think of essences, or the essential, as *that which remains the same*. Certainly, this is how other critical twentieth-century French writers have criticized the concept of essence, regarding Western metaphysics as produced through a commitment to essence. Jacques Derrida, for example, argued that the act of *meaning*, of saying that something *is*, requires that we maintain its identity through time, and that the constitution of an ongoing essence or grounding presence is therefore what underpins the history of Western thought.[8] We regard various statements and experiences through time as being the same, the same experience of the same common world. Luce Irigaray also argued that essentialism or the commitment to an abiding presence, which the subject experiences as the same, allows for a 'man' who defines himself as the knower and representing origin of that which is merely a passive ground for active thinking.[9] In both cases, essentialism signals a certain failure to think the *difference* of the world. Essences and essentialism appeared to be a tyrannizing manoeuvre of a Western thought that wishes to reduce what is other than itself to a stable, manageable and *timeless* presence. By contrast, an essence for Deleuze – contrary to usual definitions – is not what remains the same through time. There can only be time, or the production of the new, and the creation of difference, *because* there are essences: powers that create difference. Imagine if we really accepted an anti-essentialist position: that the world has no intrinsic character and that we could construct and differentiate the world according to our own interests. If that were so, then thought would have no true outside, and history would merely be a variation of one human experience. If, however, there were powers that were irreducible to the way in which they were actualized by human thought then experience would be radically shocked by its encounters. If, for example, one considered colour as the way in which the eye engages with light, one could also imagine how the differing waves of light might be experienced by an inhuman perception. Perhaps this is what colourism in art achieves; we do not just see the resulting colour but experience the lights, intensities and differences that compose colour. We see an essence of *this* singular colour that has the power to differ, eternally, according to the relations it encounters. An essence is what allows for invention, creation or time in its true sense, a time of change not a time of sameness.[10]

Accordingly, the essence of cinema, for Deleuze, is not what cinema generally or usually is. The essence of cinema is what cinema *might be*: its power or potential. We could produce films that were adaptations of books, or that adapted the styles of other art forms (biography, drama, musical performance, spy fiction). Alternatively, one could take what is *singular* in cinema, which is not what makes it the same in all its forms but what allows it to produce *new forms*, to be the essence of cinema. If, with each of its exercises the camera altered the relations among its connecting images – if it varied itself *cinematically* – then cinema would have achieved its essence, would have found its own way of difference. And this is precisely what Deleuze does in his cinema books; he looks at the ways in which different styles are produced according to the ways in which cinematic images, shots and frames are connected. *An essence is a potential for divergent connections*, a power to produce different connections. Potential is not, then, an ability added on to what something is (so that we can define cinema and say that it *might also* be revolutionary, or define thinking and say that it *might also* be creative); cinema is only cinema in its revolutionary potential, a potential to transform the ways in which perception orders its images, and thinking is only thinking when it is creative, when it does not repeat the already formed and recognized. Even when it does not actualize this potential for difference maximally – when, for example, we watch a banal Hollywood remake that resists altering the original form – cinema's radical potential is covered over, rather than absent. Any repetition, because it is a repetition *of* something that is not itself, is also the production of a difference; one can either play down this difference or push it to its limit. Cinema is only truly or essentially cinema when it does what it can do, when it is pushed to exhaustion.

Cinema, Deleuze acknowledges, more often than not does not achieve its essence, but it has at rare moments displayed its true and essential power. As a technology cinema has the power to free human life from its own tendencies. The human encounter with cinema bears the possibility of liberating the human from itself. In contrast with the idea of a history in which humanity arrives at its essence – becoming increasingly more rational and less subject to the vicissitudes of the inhuman – Deleuze's history is one in which inhuman powers, such as the power of cinema, transform the ongoing sameness and recognition of humanity, to the point where the human becomes nothing more than a power *not* to perceive itself as the same through time. Insofar as humanity is a technology – a regularity of action and perception – cinema at its most radical is a perversion of that technology. When we say that in cinema a technology allows for the passage from the human to the inhuman, we do not mean that humanity loses its essential spirit and becomes robot-like, mechanized and inhuman in the sense of being devoid of life. On the contrary, humanity has traditionally tended to ossify and reify life, fixing it into ever more regular and repeatable units. Cinema, although it also cuts reality into sections and then recomposes it into a framed whole, has two revolutionary powers. First, by bringing this segmentation to the fore 'we' can finally see what humanity was doing all along, acting as a 'spiritual automaton' or seeing machine, reducing its world to closed and manageable sets. Second, the cuts of cinema can come into direct conflict with the human eye; the camera's eye liberates us from the technology of our own bodies, finally allowing for inhuman life. We no longer see the world from the point of view of an interested and habituated body; we perceive images as such. Eventually, Deleuze argues, such technologies enable an image of time itself or the thought of time in its pure state.

SPACE AND TIME

One of the main challenges of Deleuze's thought, and one which sets him apart from the more critical approaches of other thinkers of his generation, is just this commitment to thinking life *beyond* its humanized and already constituted forms. To begin to make sense of this difference of Deleuze's thought we can begin from a crude opposition. Immanuel Kant's *Critique of Pure Reason* (1781) demonstrated that striving to think the genesis of experience was irresponsible; we can only know the world as it is experienced, and 'our' experience takes certain necessary forms – a space that results from positing the world as outside us, and a time that allows us to think of experience as continuing, and as being the experience *of* an abiding 'I'. To a certain extent Deleuze's contemporaries accepted Kantian responsibility; any appeal to a foundation or 'outside' of thought must take place from within thought. Jacques Derrida radicalized this by arguing that Kant's forms of time and space were themselves effected or made possible by forces we cannot grasp. Time is only possible if moments are marked out as the same, and space is only possible once we have a coherent scene of time. We can only think *after* time and space have been effected, but we can never grasp this genesis of space and time; thought cannot grasp its own origin, can never be present to itself. Every text of philosophy is therefore blind to its originating condition.[11]

Deleuze, however, follows Henri Bergson rather than Kant. It is true, Bergson acknowledged, that we only know the world as it is synthesized in time and space, and also true that time and space are intertwined in our perception. But this does not mean that we cannot step back from our constituted and synthesized world and intuit *how* it was synthesized, and then – further – imagine a world that might be synthesized differently. Instead of 'seeing' time as the sequence of similar events continuing in a series in which one moment is like another and can therefore be set in a spatial line, we can think time in its pure state, where time is never the same as 'itself', cannot be distributed spatially into separate points. Each creative change or difference in life opens a different time or 'duration'. It is true, for example, that I can think of my life as being the life *of* this person who is much like any other person and who therefore has a place *in* history. Or, I could think of each perceiving person's life as a constantly differing flow; I am not the same as I was a few moments ago, and the changes I will undergo depend on the specific and singular changes I have already undergone; my memory is a constantly altering and open whole, with each new experience also altering what counts as my past, but my past also altering the ways in which I change. Not only is each person a specific duration; there are also, for Bergson, inhuman durations. We do not just move around in a world which we manipulate at our will; the world has its own movements, all with different speeds. This can take extremely banal forms, as when I have to wait for a change in the world outside me, such as the time it takes for sugar to dissolve in my coffee. But the thought of different durations can be profound. We could begin to think of other cultures, not as earlier or more primitive versions of our own, but as occupying another style of duration, or different mode of temporality. We could also, within Western culture, consider 'man' to be the image of a body that has progressed *through time* while gaining more and more information; *or*, we could think of 'becoming-woman' as another style of duration, where instead of there being an image – that exists within time – we think of 'woman' as one who must create herself through connections and images, and thereby opening time.[12]

If we take duration seriously then each flow of creative time has a present that is qualitatively different according to the specific way in which it has become. Such differences are made particularly apparent in contemporary Australian political negotiations between the government and indigenous Australians regarding sacred land. Australian Aborigines have made claims to occupy land on the basis that their present identity is constituted through a spiritual affiliation with an earth, an earth that bears a sacredness because of its history. History, for Aboriginal peoples, is not a history of documents or a legal and political archive, but a 'dreaming' or body of myths concerning human and animal bodies. For this reason the last decade of the twentieth century witnessed a series of claims on the part of Aboriginal peoples, who argued both that their land had been taken illegally and that their current life was threatened by a loss of land that they could not simply regard as matter or property. Australian government responses tended to recognize land claims, however, only if the use of land would be viable and economically responsible. What appeared at the surface as a conflict between two groups was, and remains, a dispute about durations: on the one hand a time and a people whose memory is given through a virtually present collective memory and land, and on the other hand a time of European culture measured by a 'man' who remains the same regardless of locale and for whom land and culture are external items of property. For Deleuze, philosophy only begins to think when it encounters these other durations, other unfoldings of time which *never* take the form of a single line or development.

Bergson's late work defined humanity as a capacity for spirit to intuit durations beyond those of its immediate interest and appropriation.[13] Morality, he argued, begins from an interested and functional tendency to utility; we form communities and recognize others as similar to us, and this minimizes conflict and aids efficiency. But this tendency may be extended in the spiritual or religious attitude, where we recognize the duration of others not present to us, and not for any end they might serve. When we extend a tendency beyond utility we eventually arrive at its essence, transformed beyond its initial interest; in the case of morality, we eventually look beyond those who are like us and with whom we can empathize, to humanity in general. We arrive at religion or the spiritual. It is this capacity for intuiting durations beyond immediate self-interest (and, for Deleuze, beyond the human) that Deleuze emphasizes in his book on Bergson, and that also features in the history of capitalism he wrote with Félix Guattari. Rather than consider 'man' as a being who goes through time, such that time would be homogenized from the point of view of a single humanity, Deleuze and Guattari look at the ways in which 'man' is formed through a process of increasing generality and homogenization, with primitive and specific assemblages of bodies eventually forming a single body (of humanity) that commands a time that is always and everywhere of the same form and measure. That is, it may be the case that something like a territory or grouping of human bodies allows life to develop, but there also comes a point (such as late capitalism) when the image of 'man' or the 'subject' blocks the development of thinking. In such cases we need to intuit the tendencies of forces from which 'man' arose, and then extend those tendencies beyond the human animal. In their work on capitalism and schizophrenia Deleuze and Guattari argue that their geology of life – their study of the forces[14] and connections from which the social world has emerged – will allow for a reactivation of those forces beyond the restrictive image of humanity as a labouring, consuming and upright 'man' of reason.[15]

For Deleuze, the essence of cinema *when thought through fully or when pushed to its limit*, discloses a perception of life even more radical than that posed by Bergson. In what follows we can see the ways in which Deleuze locates his argument about cinema in a broader philosophy of life. We already have to be careful of reducing Bergson to a simple vitalism, or determination of all history from an original and unified expansive tendency; for Bergson it is the very *creative* power of life which will issue in divergent and unpredictable ends, not reducible to the achievement of an aim or end.[16] Deleuze, while committed to the *immanence* of thought – not simply adopting a standard or measure to which life or thought will be submitted – nevertheless stresses that there are powers or potentials of life, such as those released in cinema or philosophy, that allow creative potential to be approached in itself, without this potential being seen as the potential *of* some being. The very fact that Deleuze takes this path – thinking cinema in terms of life and life in terms of cinema – indicates the profound nature of his philosophy. Philosophy, for Deleuze, is, not surprisingly, an art of thinking; but thinking must not just happen. Thinking forces itself to take place and can only do so through encountering what is not itself. The happy repetition of what we already know – communicating agreeably and logically – is *not* thinking at its most profound. Deleuze is, on the one hand, resistant to defining his concepts through everyday or commonsense examples; but he is also insistent that philosophy's elevation of an upright and benevolent 'image of thought' is at odds with life.[17] Life's power is best expressed and evidenced, not in the general and everyday, nor in the normative, but in the perverse, singular and aberrant (for this is when life exposes its creative and diverging power, not the illusion of sameness which we require for utility).

In looking at events within life, such as cinema, and asking how such events might help us to *think*, Deleuze already makes an acute methodological decision regarding philosophy. We do not apply philosophy to cinema – asking whether a film or form is 'ethical' or 'thoughtful' – nor do we simply use cinema for examples, looking for narratives or images that demonstrate the point we want to make. We ask how cinema is possible – what is life such that it can yield cinematic technology? – and we ask what the possibilities of cinema are: how might we perceive and think differently in the face of cinematic images, and what does this tell us about the power of thinking to transform itself? What is life such that it can create cinematic images and then think those images in a philosophy that creates concepts? We can make these questions more clear by retracing Deleuze's pathway through cinema, via his own reading of Bergson. Rather than remain within cinema we will try to see how Deleuze's style of thought enables new thoughts and practices. The books on cinema are not examples of good thinking; they demonstrate *one* of the ways in which thought can deviate from exemplarity.

BERGSON, TIME AND LIFE

Bergson, like so many thinkers of his time,[18] saw thought as irreducibly historical *and* as having arrived at a point in its history when it could recognize itself and traverse its own tendency.

> [O]ur brain, our society, and our language are only the external and various signs of one and the same internal superiority. They tell, each after its manner, the unique, exceptional success which life has won at a given moment of its evolution. They express the difference of kind, and not only of degree, which separates man from the rest of the animal world. They let us guess that, while at the end of the vast spring-board from which life has taken its leap, all the others have stepped down, finding the cord stretched too high, man alone has cleared the obstacle.[19]

That is, by no longer being subject to the illusion that there is a timeless and unchanging humanity, and by confronting its historical dimensions, human life could think time far more radically. All those structures which 'we' once took to be timeless and inhuman – the truths of science – could now be recognized as creations of a humanity that abstracts from the fluxes of time to produce an enduring tradition. Along with thinkers like Edmund Husserl, whose arguments about the emergence of timeless sense *from time* were crucial for Deleuze's *The Logic of Sense*, Bergson also conducted a critique of the physical sciences.[20] Science is an abstractive process, which creates generalities that remain the same through time, and which then allows the world to be managed and mastered. The intellect perceives the world of matter as *extended* or as fully *actual*; the changes we might make to the world of matter (by cutting it up, redistributing it, reorganising it) do not change what matter is, and remain predictable and measurable. By contrast, the *life* of the intellect – its creative or spiritual energy – is *intensive* and virtual; minds, for example, are not the same through time, and their position and movement through the world is qualitatively different according to their specific time and trajectories. Each mind has its own memory, and forms a perceptive opening on to the world. Spiritual or creative manifolds are *intensive* precisely because their division would create what is *not* already given, what is virtual. At its simplest, I cannot on the basis of the last twenty years of my life predict how the next twenty will be; this is not just because I encounter other predictable durations, but because I do not know the form my own duration will take, whether my desires will remain the same, whether one change or one thought might transform the very style of my thinking. One of the main problems for Bergson is that we have tended to perceive mind according to the *extended* and *actual* forms of matter; we have human sciences that look at mind as a relatively stable object within time which one could measure from one moment to another. We also tend on a day-to-day level to treat ourselves as though we were already given and fully actual: this is me. It is useful and life-serving to perceive only what interests us in what is other than ourselves, and so sciences are *intellectual* practices that minimize difference. Science takes its cue from matter. If matter – say, a stone that is affected by its outside world directly, absorbing heat, light and moisture but making nothing of what it receives – is extended, this is because extension does not relate any point in time to any other; the sun that shines on it tomorrow will have the same effect as the sun that shines today. Whereas what you tell me now will alter how I react tomorrow, and this because each experience in time renders my ongoing time different in its way of maintaining itself; what happens to matter does not alter its duration. If you repeat the same words to me tomorrow as today – whether those words are 'I love you' or 'Tidy your office' – their effect will be different; and there may even be a threshold point when a repetition will create a singular reaction:[21] I finally feel you do love me; or I simply clean my office. This is because the second time I hear those words I have already heard them once. Time, considered intensively, is therefore different at each of its moments, and cannot be considered as an accumulation of points or 'nows' that are simply added on to each other. At any moment in time one could either recall the virtual past, or imagine the virtual future – so that one's present is merely a concentrated point of an infinite and virtual open whole of time.

Matter is life at its most 'relaxed', whereas spirit is a contraction: spirit connects one moment to another, allowing for the perception of change and the experience of creative difference. The spirit that can perceive the present with a sense of the past has a degree of contraction, for it does not just locate what it perceives in space, but sees this space as given through time and having certain qualities. This degree of contraction comes to the fore in genuine memory. If I perceive this sunset, not with the scientific intellect that would recognize its physical laws and regard it as the same as any sunset, but with spirit, I would both notice its singularity – *this sunset here and now*. I would have unique and intensive memories (virtual, not present) which would mark it as different from all the other sunsets. The present is genuinely temporal only because it contracts a past at various levels. I can perceive this world in terms of what occurred yesterday, last week, or in my childhood; and my present would be different according to just which layer of my past I drew upon. It is in this sense that spirit differs with its division; each point in the past would open a new world of the present.

At the background of Bergson's argument is a striving to understand the *genesis* of thought. Why does thought emerge from life? The answer has to do with creative energy. All life is the exertion or spending of energy; any movement or propulsion forward – any creation – exerts or explodes energy. Life, by definition, strives to further or maintain itself, and must create when it encounters what is not itself. The micro-organism must form a defence from the intrusion of light; the larger organism must act when faced with cold or hunger. (To a certain extent this model of life explains the primacy of 'connection' in Deleuze and Guattari's description of desire; there are not lives that *then* have desires upon which they act. Rather, there are desiring flows that connect with other flows – eye and light – and these connections form relatively stable points. Desire is this potential for flow and connection.) This creative force of life also bears a contrary tendency of non-exertion, conservation or reduction of expenditure. We can take perception as an example. The eye could take in vast influxes of difference, with no two moments of what it perceives being the same. Every perception would confront the eye–brain with an exhausting complexity. Such a 'pure perception' can be imagined only as a limit, for each perception is always received by some specific point of view, so a selection or contraction has already been made; but one can imagine an image of God who sees all things from all points all at once and for whom, therefore, there would be duration or ongoing full creation, but no extension – no system of points within which perception took its orientation. The eye that perceived a full and complete difference would not be able to act efficiently, and would have to invent a concept for each different flux and variation. In practice, the eye selects only what interests the body within which it is located. Further, it does not respond in an immediate and fluid way to the images it encounters – in the way, for example, that waves of light and heat directly illuminate and warm a stone, or influxes of sound might *cause* a simple organism to retreat. The human eye–brain complex fixes the images it receives into an object that remains the same through time – seeing the images it encounters *as* this or that – and then decides, pauses or hesitates as to how it will act.

There is then a definitive speed of perception: the eye must ignore some differences in order to act efficiently but must also delay acting immediately in order to give what it sees some form of order or concept. Human consciousness or mind is produced in the delay or interval between being affected by an image and acting; the more we delay the more we think, but the more we have thought – the more concepts we have formed – the more quickly we are able to act. Consciousness is a slowing down or delay, rendering us different from the matter – such as rocks – which is affected immediately by the light that warms it or the fluid that erodes it. This slowing down or dura-tion of mind is enabled by contraction – which allows the past to be carried over into the present. The energy of saving perceptions from the past (contraction) allows the mind to act more efficiently, with less thought (relaxation). But if this contraction of memory becomes habitual, requiring less and less effort, we also find that the mind comes closer to matter, becoming extended or relaxed to the point of inertia. In both *The Creative Mind* and *Creative Evolution* Bergson shows the way mind emerges by slowing down, so that it can perceive images with the virtual wealth of memory and anticipation, but he also shows how such memories and functions become habitual to the point where mind starts to take on the relaxed mode of matter – treating itself as a thing that remains the same through time and is subject to a pre-given logic. The only way out would be more intense contraction. If, for example, I want to learn something new I do not just rely on efficient habits; I might have to remember not just this or that action, but what it is to learn a new action. For example, I will never be able to move efficiently in the water if I rely only on my ability to walk, walking more and more in the hope that one day I might be able to swim. I will only learn to swim if I draw upon the creative energy that I drew upon when I learned to walk. Human per-ception and time is structured by action; we can act and make our way in the world only by reducing the difference of time to a coher-ent temporal succession, by seeing objects that follow each other or move within a stable framed scene which we view at a practical dis-tance. But both Bergson and Deleuze insist that we can also liberate ourselves from the eye–brain–body complex that is oriented to action, and it is this liberation that they will define as metaphysics (Bergson) or thinking (Deleuze).

It is the *conserving tendency of life*, the tendency to reduce complexity for the sake of action (where action is understood as what is repeatable and manageable for a human body) which explains why we have a certain image of thought. We think of the world as a set of fixed objects, located in space, capable of moving within space. And as an object moves from one point in space to another the human mind observes this change from its own fixed position. Time is, therefore, defined as the measure of movement. Space is an already given, already present, field of equivalent points. If we were to consider space *intensively* however, according to duration, we would have to see space changing according to the movements it maps.[22] There is, after all, no really neutral medium *within which* movement takes place, as all space is composed of forces; this applies both to the physical universe where we can measure different fields in the solar system, and to human life where we live space intensively. Whereas Euclidean geometry measured a space where each point was the same, geometry after the formulation of differential calculus was capable of measuring a space of speeds and slowness, where, for example, a curve might have a very slow rate of change but then become more and more acute.[23] We can think of the lived universe as being far more measurable in such terms: if an architect were simply to impose a blueprint on a space then she may encounter all sorts of technical difficulties, but if she were to consider the way the land upon which she builds has a certain resistance at some points and a certain porosity at others then she would be working with space intensively, considering its own flows and responses.[24] The same applies to the human body's relation to clock time and measured space. If, for example, I run a marathon, then the last mile is not only slower (taking longer in terms of clock time) but also introduces changes of fatigue and motion in the body; the undulations in the pavement and the hills have a greater force and effect than they did in the first five miles. The final minutes of a marathon are composed of thousands of tiny perceptions – each step, each ache, each spasm increases exponentially – whereas the first half-hour might yield no perceptible change in the body. Any marathon runner knows that a marathon does not consist of four ten-kilometre runs, for the last quarter of the marathon carries the memory of the previous three.

It is not just that we homogenize time by reducing it to space, seeing the flowing complex changes of duration in terms of a line of fixed points, measuring our life out in a unit that allows one point to be equivalent to another. It is also the case that the space we have mapped on to time is a space devoid of intensity, devoid of differing speeds and dimensions. It is a certain need of life, a need to homogenize and reduce complexity, that leads to the spatialization of time, the reduction of time *and* space to the measure of movement of an unchanging unit across an unchanging series of points, the point being an abstraction from fluxes or alterations (for in reality there is no point of pure stillness, indifference or unchanging presence).

The standardization of time means that all hours and days are the same, and that we work nine to five, regardless of the different distributions of light and dark. We also regard the one hour we sleep as the same as the one hour we spend watching television (even if, in that sleeping hour, we have a dream that allows for so much influx of the past that we are never the same again and our lives take on a radically different trajectory); the hour we spend viewing paintings in a gallery is the same as the hour we spend on the treadmill in the morning (even if the hour running has introduced changes into our body that allow us to think more quickly, or tire us to the point where we are incapable of viewing the fragment of history in the painting before us). If Bergson was part of a modernist resistance to the homogenization of time,[25] he was also crucial in allowing for a realization of the complicity between time and capitalism. The more functional our measurement of time – the more clocks are synchronized to allow for one efficiently mechanized and working world – the more the idea of time *wasted* becomes an impossibility. Our leisure is no longer spent unproductively, merely allowing time to pass; even in the hours after work we are allowing production, homogenization and the uniformity of time to continue. We watch television in blocks of one hour (viewing commercials), desire products that will 'save time' and allow us to be more efficient; if we desire luxuries these take the form of designer labels so that we turn ourselves into walking Nike or Louis Vuitton advertisements. On the one hand, Bergson's resistance to the homogenization of time was critical of this tendency towards the reduction of the world to one system of efficiency; on the other hand, his appeal to a *spiritual* overcoming of the reification of time has already itself become one more industry. Capitalism and postmodernism both celebrate the consumption of leisure, creativity and individual difference.[26] What Deleuze strives to do is maintain Bergson's modernist resistance to the spatialization of time, while recognizing that art will need to do more than retrieve a lived, human time.

Deleuze's appeals to art in all its forms celebrate a modernism that does not *represent* time but opens a power to perceive time differentially. Hollywood cinema may be dominated by characters who move through time and achieve desired ends, and we may watch such films in order to spend time. Modernist cinema, by contrast, does not present time as a series of images but gives us images of a non-homogenized time, not a time of units but a time of fluctuations.[27] And this character of modernist aesthetics also pervades modernist literature. Whereas pre-modernist narratives expressed a developing time, with narratives tending towards conclusion and fulfilment, modernist novels aimed to present a time 'out of joint'[28] or 'time in its pure state',[29] where a memory may flood in, or a perception might occur, such that the present is deprived of its sense and continuity. Plot, or the future as the resolution and achievement of the past, is undone in favour of an inhuman time, a time that disturbs habit, for we perceive time not as it is for us – a general, recognized and functioning humanity – but time as a potential for difference.

Bergson's concept of duration is therefore a *concept* in Deleuze and Guattari's quite strict sense. Philosophers create concepts. The creation of a concept does not label a generality – marking out all occurrences of x *as* 'x' – for this would be *extensive*; a concept would cover or include a set of instances. Concepts, for Deleuze and Guattari, are intensive; they make connections among changes or fluxes that, in turn, allow thought to move or differ: 'Concepts are centres of vibrations, each in itself and every one in relation to all others.'[30] The concept of duration, for example, creates a thought of time that connects creation, memory, differential space, speeds and singularity; and once we have this concept – once we think of time as durations of different speeds and becomings – we can then intuit durations other than our own. From the experience of our own duration, by thinking of the ways in which the mind alters as it goes through time, we can go on to intuit other durations, and then think duration as such.

Intuition, then, is a method that enables mind, which has been composed from tendencies of life, to discern tendencies in their pure form.[31] Even though time is always experienced in our spatially extended world in terms of some sort of generalizing method, this ought not to deter us from intuiting time as it is in itself, and this can be achieved only if we free thought from its ready-made habits and its tendency towards imagining itself according to the material world fixed by the intellect. The method of intuition, which distinguishes the forces that make up any experienced composite, is, in Deleuze's work, extended far beyond Bergson's already radical metaphysical endeavours. Deleuze's entire oeuvre is dominated by a striving to *think* singularities: not the organized, managed, synthesized wholes which allow us to act efficiently and continue being ourselves, but those inhuman powers or *potentials* from which organized forms have emerged: 'A world already envelops an infinite system of singularities selected through convergence. Within this world, however, individuals are constituted which select and envelop a finite number of the singularities of the system.'[32] Whereas Bergson's project of intuiting inhuman relations focused on life in the sense in which it is usually understood – the life of the animate universe, a life that would be recognized by most theorists of evolution – the events Deleuze seizes upon that would allow us to free time from human action are resolutely inhuman. Cinematic forces, or the power for a machine to connect and redistribute images, are not representations of life; they allow a power of life to become evident to the human brain. Life, for Deleuze, goes well beyond the biological or natural sphere and includes tendencies to deviation, perversion or spiritualization: the virtual is not just, as it was for Bergson, the pure past of one cosmic memory, but is also the potential for connections that are fruitless, unproductive, divergent and singular. One example of Deleuzean intuition would be his approach to cinema, which first separates the image-composing technology of cinema from the meaning of the final film. The very possibility of a visual image being linked, cut and re-connected in lines that are not those of any moving or acting body liberates the image from the sensory-motor apparatus. So the first stage of intuition is to move back from the film to the images from which it is composed. The next stage of intuition is to return to the composite – the pure image and the human viewer – but now with the thought of the distinct forces. The cinema books therefore look at how these two forces work: what happens when the human viewer encounters an image machine.

Similarly, Deleuze's book on Proust looks at a literary work and its specific style, and distinguishes this from the ideas or philosophy expressed by the work, just as his work with Guattari on Kafka looks at the 'literary machine' or the styles Kafka used to tear the social whole into components and then show those components in different configurations. This is quite different from a philosophy of the novel, or a philosophy that uses novelistic examples. Once Deleuze shows how literary techniques work, he then discerns the way in which a literary work can demand new concepts from a philosopher. Life is a crucial concept for Deleuze, but it is a concept that is created with a quite different intension from that of Bergson. In their book on Kafka, Deleuze and Guattari define life, neither as some context within which a literary work is located, nor as the biography of the writer, but as a concept enabled by what Kafka's novels *do*. Kafka uses all sorts of images – animals, machines and courtrooms – to re-create connections. The courtroom of *The Trial* is not a realistic representation but is an intensification of the sort of life, the sorts of desires and connections, from which courts, government departments and modern institutions eventually emerged. By 'life', then, Deleuze and Guattari refer to Kafka's art of decomposing the *actual* political context in order to see the movements from which the specific context emerges:

> The creative line of escape vacuums up in its movement all politics, all economy, all bureaucracy, all judiciary: it sucks them like a vampire in order to make them render still unknown sounds that come from the near future – Fascism, Stalinism, Americanism, *diabolical powers that are knocking at the door*. Because expression precedes content and draws it along (on the condition, of course, [that it] is nonsignifying: living and writing, art and life, are opposed only from the point of view of a major literature.[33]

Their concept of 'minor literature' is therefore defined in conjunction with the radical concept of life. If life is not just the actual world, but also all its virtual potentials, then a minor literature will be great in its capacity to think of life not as it *is* – what we all know – but what it might *become*: life from new points of view.[34]

Deleuze's concept of 'life' makes connections among the brain, images, memory and the productions of art, science and philosophy. If such productions exist, then this must tell us about life's power to produce such divergent 'lines'. Philosophy and art are not representations or images *of* life, but we can understand something of life's creative potential if we consider the emergence or genesis of art and philosophy. If we *intuit* the forces that produce any single work of art or any single concept, then we might begin to approach singularity as such: the power of making a difference. Like Bergson, Deleuze insists that we should interrogate the genesis of *any* organized body or relatively closed form – including the bodies of humans, societies, art, philosophy and science – and move to the 'body without organs', or the forces from which bodies are composed, and then finally to the thought of life as such (that which differs in force). Whereas Bergson's account referred back to a dynamic open whole of creatively evolving life that eventually (but contingently) arrives at a human form capable of intuiting its own genesis (Bergson, 1911), Deleuze places far greater emphasis on inhuman events, inorganic life and (what Deleuze and Guattari refer to in *Anti-Oedipus* as) anti-production, or the power of life to turn against itself, or *not* express its full power.

Bergson's intuited inhuman durations were most often exemplified by other animate or at least natural forms, such as the time taken for sugar to dissolve in liquid – so that the life in general of creative evolution was a natural life, with technology considered to be parasitic. (Bergson saw the cinematic snapshot as an intensification of the already mechanizing process by which the intellect fixes reality into static images.) We reduce the world to a uniform, quantifiable mechanism. The physical sciences are (or were) dominated by a mathematical reasoning that determines the world in advance in terms of equivalent units of measure. If, however, we think of the *life* of other organisms, such as the 'world' of the animals we eat, or the earth we plunder, we will realize that *human* space, which maps the world as so much already existent useable matter, necessarily discounts other durations; we act as if what is other than ourselves remains the same, bearing no intrinsic relations. 'Our' history occurs as a single line, with the earth being the medium or backdrop for human action. Today, our manipulation of 'resources' brings us up against other times, not just the inhumanly slow formation that produces fossil fuels over millennia that can then be exhausted in hundreds of years, but also the speeds of inhuman durations that can produce mutations, divergences and extinctions within our lifetime. The very being of humanity is today changing at a greater speed because we are moving faster across the earth; phenomena such as bird flu can mutate and leap from pigs to humans, and then across the body of humanity, with all this being intensified by forms of travel that create faster and larger global networks of bodies. Not only is time not our own, our own time is altered by movements beyond the body of humanity.

For Bergson, there is a metaphysical imperative in the method of intuition. Only by liberating ourselves from a world reified for the purposes of efficient action, and only by perceiving what a world might be for an organism not in tune with our own rhythms, will we too recognize that we have a specific but forgotten duration and that this is a duration capable of concentrating not just on its own present and memory, but the memory and intuitions of those not present – humanity in general.[35] We can move from the perception of an autumnal leaf falling from a tree, to the farmed soil upon which that leaf falls, and then across to a lake where humans playing on a jet-ski disturb the lake's fish. Such a perception is at once located within the human point of view, but also allows for distinct rhythms, durations and imagined points that are beyond the human: the yearly cycles of the natural and agricultural seasons, the broader timescale of an earth and sea that have altered ecologies because of human action, and the times of other human beings who go about their daily work and play. This is *not* the time of Einstein's relativity theory, which for Bergson only goes *some* way towards understanding that clock time is a homogenizing abstraction. We can only have a theory of relativity – a sense of the different speeds that make up incommensurable durations – if there is a relativity theorist, a perceiver capable of intuiting this one life composed of different durations.[36] That is, we cannot just have a theory of relativity: the assertion or observation that time would be different for different observers in different locations, moving at different speeds. We also have to note and bear responsibility for the fact that it is possible to think or represent those different speeds; this is only possible because in addition to all the singular durations there is also a capacity – the theoretical rather than practical capacity – for thinking duration as such, the one life that gives itself in speeds and slownesses.[37] Humanity is the outcome of a creative history. We think in terms of a fixed and uniform space because we have the potential to further our own lives, but that same potential or tendency can take us one step further. Once we recognize that our fixed extended world is the outcome of our human tendency to mastery and management, we can recognize that tendency as essentially creative and *then* think of humanity not as a fixed form but as a creative principle. For, Bergson insists, the creative power that has propelled us forward, that has enabled us to see the world in our own image, is the same power that can intuit the emergence of this image. Thus, at a certain point in the history of life there emerges an event – the method of intuition – that enables a true thought of *all* life, not just its constituted human form.

CHAPTER 2

THE MOVEMENT-IMAGE

THE HISTORY OF TIME AND SPACE AND THE HISTORY OF CINEMA

Deleuze begins his first volume of *Cinema* with a historical account of the perception of space and movement:

> For antiquity, movement refers to intelligible elements, Forms or Ideas which are themselves eternal and immobile . . . Movement, conceived in this way, will thus be the regulated transition from one form to another, that is, an order of *poses* or privileged instants, as in a dance . . .
>
> The modern scientific revolution has consisted in relating movement not to privileged instants, but to any-instant-whatever. Although movement was still recomposed, *it was no longer recomposed from formal transcendental elements (poses), but from immanent material elements (sections)*. Instead of producing an intelligible synthesis of movement, a sensible analysis was derived from it.[1]

While this history of space and time does have a crucial part to play in Deleuze's understanding of the history of cinema, his history of cinema also plays a part in a broader argument regarding the significance of the image of time. As long as time is regarded as grounded upon movement (whether that be the movement of bodies towards their proper final form, or the movement of bodies across a uniform space) we will fail to see time in its pure state.

Pre-modern thought saw movement as the realization or achievement of a fixed form or pose. This was connected to a broader theory of life, where each organism essentially moves towards realizing what it properly is: humans, for example, have their proper motion in reason and become fully human only in exercising their rational potential. Each section of movement was, therefore, not equivalent. Movements were passages towards achieving a proper form and were therefore closer to, or further from, what they ought to realize. Space was the milieu in which temporal forms were realized, and movement was movement *towards* each being's proper place; there is a space and motion of heavenly bodies, a different law of space and motion for earthly bodies. To a certain extent, but without the nostalgic endorsement, Deleuze echoes a standard picture of the Aristotelian universe. Before the homogenization and scientific reduction of the world to unformed matter, each being had its proper place and mode of movement.[2] Time was defined as the time taken for such movements to realize the forms that were, essentially, unchanging. This image of a world of heterogeneous space, where each being had its intrinsic nature and order, has often been invoked sentimentally. Once upon a time the world was not yet subjected to capital, scientific reduction, quantification, disenchantment and mechanism. Deleuze, however, both refuses the idea of a *fall* into modernity and insists that a tendency to capitalism or quantification exists in pre-capitalist formations, which have ways of 'warding off' capitalism. This refusal of nostalgia depends on his commitment to immanence. Deleuze will not see capitalism (or any other supposed 'evil') as an accident that befalls life and that one might simply step outside of: if it is *possible* for the world to be reduced to equivalent, uniform, objectified and manageable matter – with change being nothing more than the circulation of the already given, and production being the maximization and increase of quantity – then this is because there is a tendency in life towards organization, as well as a counter-tendency towards dis-organization. (We will keep returning to this broad thesis of tendencies and stratification, with one flow producing relative stability and a counter-flow that resists closure and opens out to difference.) In the background of the two books on cinema there is a quite subtle argument regarding time, money and humanity. Capitalism appears to be an event that turns the flows of individual lives, our own desires and meanings, into a single global present: time is money. Everything we do is quantified, including the leisure time we buy by paying for time-saving services, or by spending on time-diverting activities.

One dominant motif that will run throughout Deleuze's early work and his work with Guattari is that of privatization, which helps to explain abstract time, capitalism, meaning, sexuality and subjectivity. Privatization is the formation of a flow that has no specific or collective meaning, that is the same whether it is mine or yours, has no sense, locus or identity *and becomes what it is only with appropriation*. Time, in capitalism, is privatized; every hour is the same as every other, and I can buy more of my own time by hiring childminders, personal assistants, researchers, life-coaches and someone to talk to on a chat-line. There is no sense that I have to spend my own time in doing these things in order to be the person I am; privatization is complete when I can buy everything – from sex to personal style – that defines me as who I am. There can be private property only if something has no *proper* place or being and can circulate freely to become mine or yours. Money brings the tendency to privatization to its most explicit form by creating a single flow that recognizes no difference as it circulates; there can only be private property if the matter of the world has no intrinsic quality or tendency and can be distributed and appropriated. As Deleuze and Guattari argue in *Anti-Oedipus*, even the psyche is privatized. Images that were once lived collectively – such as the despot who is feared by all – are displaced by the relation each subject in capitalism has to his own conscience or internalized father-figure. We can now go to psychoanalysis and pay to have our own private neuroses managed. But even though capitalism and the monetary system are intensifications of privacy, there are tendencies to privatization in primitive life. Deleuze and Guattari explain the way collective investments in the body – the tribal phallus, the totems of the eye or breast, the sacred fluids of blood – produce quite specific territories, or styles of assembled bodies. A proto-form of privatization occurs with the anus, which is not displayed publicly or given any form of collective investment; shit becomes meaningless, inhuman waste – not mine, not yours, not owned. What this evidences is a tendency in life towards a circulation or flow liberated from any body proper, freed from organization or proper place. When capitalism posits our private individuality, sexuality and subjectivity – such that we are nothing more than the labour we sell, the products we buy and the fantasies we take into our hearts – it extends a potential of time as such, a potential for organization and axioms. The flow of time is productive, creating forms and flows; but it is always possible that one of those forms or flows – such as money – will be taken as the measure of time.

In tracing the genesis of modern capitalism as both a deterritorialization allowing for greater freedom of flows, and an axiomatic whereby all flows are part of one system of time, Deleuze and Guattari will seize on a number of modern events that might provide a break with capitalism's reterritorializations. For the Deleuze of the cinema books, cinema is both part of a history of the reduction of time to movement and measure *and* a way of thinking beyond the quantification of time. This is why his cinema books are historical in a quite specific sense, for each cinematic form will be a way of relating images of spatial movement to images of time. By the time cinema emerges as a form, we have already abandoned an Aristotelian universe where each form has its proper space and proper movement. The pre-modern understanding of space as a site for the realization of pre-given forms, and time as the irrelevant but necessary passage to those forms, *is* different from the modern understanding of a uniform, quantifiable and abstract space and a derivative, merely subjective and private time (even if what they share is a tendency towards measuring time with time's own productions, and the tendency to reduce production to the maximization of efficient flows *within* time, rather than the creation of proliferating durations). With modern scientific conceptions of space and time there is both a tendency towards a true thought of time and life, *and* a concomitant retreat from modern science's radical potential. Indeed, what characterizes Deleuze's history of philosophy and Deleuze and Guattari's histories of life is an insistence on radical change (time) that has always borne the potential for joyful life, even though these potential becomings have yet to realize their revolutionary force. Deleuze's history of cinema is no exception, as cinema also harbours a potential to transform the brain's relationship to an image of thought, even though this transformation is anything but inevitable. Everything in Deleuze affirms the *chance* of becoming: events of change are truly possible but this is precisely because they are also neither likely nor inevitable, and certainly not already given in present conditions.

In the case of the modern rethinking of space, there is at once a liberation of space from the realization of forms. Space is no longer oriented towards intrinsic forms, and movement is neither the passage from one essentially distinct place to another, nor a particular mode of movement. Any point in a movement is equivalent to any other.

We can measure a section of a trajectory in terms of all other sections, with the space it occupies being 'any-space-whatever'. Now, there is a radical potential opened here, for movement is no longer oriented in advance to what it ought to achieve, and space is no longer governed by pre-given and timeless forms. Space is no longer an already determined order that would govern movement; movement is not movement towards some goal that is its reason. As a consequence there is the possibility of thinking a becoming or passage that is not determined in advance, a becoming that might yield an event: a trajectory that does not have its end within itself. The 'any-space-whatever' of modernity is, however, domesticated by a derivative understanding of time. Far from movement enabling or producing change – far from time or becoming being that which propels each movement differently according to the forces it traverses – time becomes the measure of movement. There are several ways we can think of this subordination. The first is through the history of science and philosophy. If we think of movement extensively and metrically, then each point in the movement takes the same form and speed as any other. We view space and movement through a Euclidean geometry of flat space, equivalent points and straight lines. If, however, as the seventeenth-century philosopher Leibniz (1646–1716) began to do, we try to think of curves and differential speeds (accelerations and decelerations) then we begin to approach space intensively and non-metrically. A curve 'speeds up' as it becomes more acute, slows down as it levels out. Whereas the *completed* trajectory would represent all points at once, capable then of being calculated at an average speed, the trajectory in its real duration is uneven, covering more space and altering more for some time, traversing less space and remaining relatively uniform as the curve levels out. As the history of physics and mathematics develops, the very homogenization of space that reduced time – where all points in space are given all at once and equivalent to all others, and time is nothing more than the passage from one point to another – allows for a radical encounter with time. If space is not determined in advance by a proper order, and if movement is really possible, then *movements will alter space*, not just take place in space. A movement may create new dimensions, produce different fields, and in so doing will not be a rearrangement of some already given whole mapped by time, but will create a difference in what is, and will then open new durations. If I travel to another culture and learn its history, and that culture in turn learns my history, then the past that we now have is of a larger world, which then opens the possibility for a quite different future; we will not act in the same ways, nor think the same way. On the one hand such an argument is merely metaphorical, for of course we inhabited the same world all along and we now only become aware of each other's histories; but on the other hand there is a quite specific sense of worlds opening up in time, through time, that Deleuze will continually reinforce. The world, life, in its fullest sense, comprises all those worlds of located perceivers. If I encounter another perceiver whose world makes an entirely different set of connections from my own, and if the encounter opens up a new culture, this will still harbour the potential – virtual but unactualized – for other encounters, other collisions of time and other worlds that would all be expressions of one 'cosmic memory' (held by no one individual). If we can think of movement, not as a shift of a body across space and in time, but as a movement of force, traversing other forces, then time and space will be open wholes.

It is the conception of movement across 'any-space-whatever' that Deleuze seizes upon in the movement-image of classical cinema. There are two tendencies in the modern space of any-space-whatever. The first is a space and time subordinated to a privileged point of view such that movement is always movement from point to point within a stable frame. Thus, if we take the point of view of a body oriented towards action and self-maintenance it makes sense to take the viewing point as a centre which then orients all movements as movements within its frame of reference; time would then be the necessary continuity or synthesis the viewer constitutes from one point to another. Time would be radically or transcendentally subjective, a condition or form through which something like a continuous and mapped space would be possible (and space would also be essential for this measuring or numbering of time, for without the distinction between stable observer and object observed (or inner and outer sense) there could be no point from which a continuous time could be synthesized.[3] In addition to thinking about time in this subject-centred and abstract manner, we can also extrapolate implications for narrative – implications that will be significant for Deleuze's modernist affirmation of non-narrative art and cinema. If space is an abstract field of possible points of movement, and time is the synthesis or tracing of that movement, then there is an accompanying understanding of narrative, where the end or resolution is the proper completion of a trajectory that is desired or anticipated by the interested viewer or reader. Movement has a proper end, which is the completion of an action; time is the time taken for this journey, movement or arrival to take place – a shift from situation A to situation B. In his first book on cinema, Deleuze looks at how one set of images is oriented towards the development of another, so the image we are given is one of movement and the time taken is given *indirectly* (for we are given an image of time – say, of the passage of several years or decades – but this is not time as such but only the time that passes in a transition or alteration of a situation).

The second potential of the modern space of 'any-space-whatever' is radical, for the centre of action or the point from which movement is viewed is no longer the human pragmatically driven subject but is the eye of the camera. Cinema, like any other form of narrative, can take the point of view of an elevated or epic observer – panning generations or epochs. But this potential can be extended beyond that of a single observer. This would occur if the camera were to begin to encompass nature as an evolving whole, with movements or developments that were not intended by human agents. Soviet cinema, for example, uses montage to connect movements of nature such as a severe snowstorm, with technological movements such as the invention of new factory machines, with social movements, such as a famine or depression, thereby showing the ways in which the productions of time are not just those of action or movement of mapped objects. It is this radicalization that Deleuze seizes upon in the movement-image. The movement-image presents time indirectly by connecting mobile sections, so time is not the movement of a body in space but is depicted as made up of various intersecting spaces.

THE MOVEMENT-IMAGE AND SEMIOTICS

To a great extent, Deleuze's two volumes on cinema (and the history that they narrate) is governed by a normative aesthetic which is also an ethics. In the case of the classical cinema considered in the first volume, Deleuze insists that the potential that is the *essence* of cinema – the potential to transform the structure of perception which has dominated the history of thought – is only realized in some films, and that we can mark the greatness of a cinematic author by the extent to which he or she realizes the power of the cinematic apparatus. If, for example, cinema is regarded as offering a translation or representation of reality (or some other medium such as books or plays), then cinema is only different by degree from other experiences. Films that faithfully follow a literary or dramatic text, and that try to downplay the role of cinema, work against the potential of cinema. They separate cinema from what it can do; and if there is one over-riding ethic in Deleuze's work it is this: to live up to the powers from which we are composed, to extend potentials or *life* to the *n*th power. Films that *think* in the apparatus of cinema, by contrast, are instances of an encounter. The brain is required to work, to confront the shock of a set of images no longer selected and synthesized to facilitate habitual action.

Deleuze gives a series of examples of the movement-image, all of which give an indirect image of time. In doing so he makes both a local and global point. Locally, his approach is highly formalist. The study of film should not take place through another language – trans-lating visual images into a narrative or meaning – nor operate with the assumption that film is already a language, such that cinematic images would compose a structure that would function in the same way that written or spoken discourse works (by producing a set of differences). Rather, Deleuze sees the images of cinema and, most importantly, their construction as specific to a cinematic style of thinking. His philosophy does try to give this thinking *conceptual* form, to articulate in philosophical concepts the very life of time that cinema allows us to see. His key point is that the specific technology of cinema allows for various styles of construction, and these styles are always ways of thinking. We neither apply philosophy to cinema, nor use cinema for philosophical examples; but if we *think* through cinema, then philosophical thinking will also be transformed.

From this local commitment to considering cinema cinematically – that is, in terms of how it works and not as the reproduction of a message, moral or sense that might equally well be presented in other modes – Deleuze gives us a glimpse into both his philosophy and his ethics. His philosophical method in these books is a radical empiri-cism: how does a sequence of images and its specific style of connec-tion produce ideas? How does a sense of life, a point of view upon the whole of life, emerge from within life? Deleuze's empiricism refuses to posit, as an act of faith, a mind or subject of good sense that exists in order to re-present the world. As the two volumes progress we rec-ognize a very close relationship between cinema and what Deleuze takes to be a truly ethical way of approaching any event. It is *after* the advent and brief history of cinema – if considered faithfully and without pre-given images of what counts as proper thinking – that we can then recognize that *life has always evolved creatively through the production of relations among images.* The history of thought – the history of the brain and of life – is cinematic: life is composed of relatively stable zones of perception. The human organism evolves through its editing, synthesizing and relating of images. When the human brain confronts this process of imaging, when it *thinks* cinema, it opens the possibility of thinking differently: we have, all along, operated as a 'spiritual automaton', but only when we engage with other modes of linkage, other visual machines, do we realize a potential to extend our powers of synthesis and connection. The movement-image is, for Deleuze, at once grounded in the representation of action; we see events linked according to a sequence of human purposes, of natural consequences, or of changing situations. At the same time, the movement-image, by presenting the sequence of images that allows a situation to prompt action, and from that action the creation of another situation, also yields an indirect image of time. The cinema presents those movements from which time, as an unfolding and continually altering whole, is indicated indirectly. A movement or action does not take place within a world that remains unchanged; each action alters a situation, alters relations and thereby alters the whole. Whereas everyday vision is caught up in its own actions and purposes, the cinema of the movement-image allows for the perception of movements framed by the changing whole of life. The fact that movements are connected indirectly to an 'open whole' is made possible by various styles of the cinematic apparatus.

At the level of cinematic experience and film theory, Deleuze makes one key theoretical manoeuvre. He does not read film according to external criteria, either according to themes and content – say, how a film translates a message or narrative from life or a novel – or in relation to film as a language in the narrow sense, where images would be signs of some pre-filmic content. Rather, the entirety of *Cinema 1* theorizes film's own language, its specific style or regime of signs. This has implications which go well beyond cinema. Deleuze is insistent elsewhere that we should not see signification or the system of signifiers (language in the narrow written/spoken sense) as exhaustive of signs. Every regime of signs, whether they be the signs one lover gives to another, the signs one micro-organism presents to another or the signs of a bird's refrain[4] that will mark out its territory, operates with its own particular style of difference.[5] Cinema's signs or differentia work by creating blocks of images, relating variously to time, movement and action. Cinema has signs of its own and each cinematic style or method creates new signs. Here Deleuze draws upon the semiotics of the American pragmatist C. S. Peirce (1839–1914) and he does so for well-considered philosophical reasons that go beyond any simple applicability to cinema. For Peirce there are levels of signs, with symbolic signs – the signs of a language – being grounded on icons, or images that stand for things (such as a traffic sign that depicts the image of a slippery surface), which in turn are grounded on indexes, (with smoke being the signs of fire, a bullet hole being the sign of a gunshot). The key reason for drawing upon Peirce is that signs are not seen as imposed upon life by a human mind that establishes difference and relations; rather, all life is already a plane of relating differences, establishing branching and proliferating connections:

> Difference must become the element, the ultimate unity; it must therefore refer to other differences which never identify it but rather differentiate it. Each term of the series, being already a difference, must be put into variable relations with other terms, thereby constituting other series devoid of center and convergence. Divergence and decentering must be affirmed in the series itself.[6]

Deleuze's radical empiricism or transcendental empiricism[7] is a commitment to experience: one ought not impose pre-given criteria upon experience, but ought to read, discern and intuit the principles and workings of experience from experience itself. This precludes the grounding of experience on one of its effects, such as accepting the image of common sense as the limit of experience. Rather, it entails asking what experience might be capable of given the evidence we already have of its powers. In the case of cinema and semiotics, this requires that we do not begin with some overarching transcendental condition, such as the idea that we are all submitted to a system of signification or law, and that we can only think the beyond or 'other' of this system fantasmatically. Deleuze's method is therefore in direct contrast with the cinematic theory inspired by Lacan, where the image on the screen stands in for, or covers over, that which we imagine as lost or lacking.[8] If the Lacanian theory of the image were true then we would have to accept that the eye's relation to the image is always one of signification, subjection and subordination: what does the image re-present, what does it cover over or withhold from me? To accept this scenario of signification would be to read cinema as a fantasy frame, as a staging of the trauma that situates 'us' within a logic that is radically other, and that necessarily posits a 'not-all' or 'beyond' outside the frame of images.[9] The broader background to Lacanian theory is one in which signification differentiates an undifferentiated real, in which the signifier is imposed and prohibits us from grasping the very thing in itself.[10]

For Deleuze, this semiotic approach or commitment to a symbolic order which determines the field of perception and experience in advance is an illegitimate extension of the recognition that our perceptual field is synthesised or produced.[11] Yes, we perceive our own world in connected, synthesized and unfolded series, always from some specific zone of perception, such as the human eye or body. This is the productive synthesis which is at the heart of all experience, not only human experience. We can see the way in which the eye connects its visual field, the way human bodies connect to produce groups, the way organisms connect to produce ecological synergies. But it is illegitimate to go from connection and production to an unseen but presupposed subject or 'who' that is the ground or hidden order of production. From organized bodies – assembled through connections – we can extrapolate a 'body without organs' that must have been their condition, but this will always be read back from its effects.[12] In the beginning is production, with the producer or subject being effected alongside production as the *conjunction* of all the produced connections. If any idea has enslaved thought it is this one: the movement from a series of connections and productions to an absent ground or cause which is presupposed as the law of production – whether that ground be God, 'man' or the system of signification. In the case of film theory what Deleuze, as an empiricist, objects to is the assumption of a system which is then seen to be taken up by the cinematic apparatus, such that the visual field would always be haunted by an absent other that is its cause. That is, the screen would be a frame through which we *relive* the trauma that installed us as subjects *subjected to* a fantasy of an Other who holds the cause and secret of our desire. By contrast, for Deleuze the screen is a dehumanization of the image, a scene where the visual can be freed from the local subject, and released to yield its autonomous power.

Cinematic signs cannot therefore be reduced to signs of the subject, signs of communication or signs issued by one signifying being to another. If the Lacanian mantra is that 'a signifier represents a subject for another signifier', this is because a signifier will be read as a message from another, and it is this address from the other that installs me as a subject.[13]

By contrast, Deleuze draws upon Peirce's semiotics, both to insist on the production, genesis and diversity of signs, and to *deduce* signs. That is, in keeping with empiricism and its aim of immanence (or not presupposing a transcendent condition beyond experience) Deleuze insists that we should not simply accept the existence of a system of signification but should examine how such systems emerge, work and are produced. This is where cinema comes in, and for three reasons. First, cinema works with a different regime of signs than that of spoken language. Its sign system has a different structure or different style of relations; formal languages operate by differences among terms and create universals or generalities, whereas cinematic signs operate by relations of time. Visual images produce different relations among each other, and between the image and its outside. Second, following Peirce, far from assuming a system of relations, cinema allows us to think the emergence of relations; it does not just establish itself within a symbolic order but operates with potentials and affects from which systems are produced. Third, by *not* operating at the level of already established linguistic systems – such as the system of the speaking subject, which is the result of a history that produces 'man' as an effective social animal – cinema opens the history of thought beyond the sensory-motor apparatus that has dominated the synthesis of images. We can deal with these three aspects in turn: cinema's style of images; the deduction of images from life; and the overturning of the sensory-motor apparatus. Once we do so we can see the *problem* Deleuze discerned in the advent of cinema, a problem that extends beyond cinema.

STYLES OF SIGN

In *Cinema 1: The Movement-Image* and *Cinema 2: The Time-Image* Deleuze goes through an elaborate, detailed and highly specific analysis of the different ways in which cinematic images are connected, and the ideas that such connections produce. Critical to the first book on cinema and the creation of the movement-image is the technique of montage. Deleuze looks at the way certain events of perception – the connection and cutting of images – allow us to think of life or the 'open whole'. Life is an open whole because it is at once the totality of all events and relations – a whole – but a totality that alters or has new potentials with each new relation. We have already noted Deleuze's location of cinema within a broader thesis regarding space and movement. Movement is no longer movement towards some proper pre-given goal, but at each of its moments is altering from itself. That is, movement is not subordinated to a change from one position to another; rather, the analysis of movement itself will disclose the production of change from movements. There is movement from place to place only because there is that which moves or unfolds, creating a line of time and in so doing producing a plane of relations. Sergei Eisenstein's (1898–1948) cinema, with the method of montage, creates a movement-image that enables the intuition of a movement of becoming. This is achieved by presenting movements, not as a single body moving through space, but by connecting different movements to present one changing and dynamic whole. The movement of a human body (a relation between persons) may be connected to a movement of machines (the image of a factory) and then to a social movement (a blockade); we would see movement not as change *within* space but as a changing whole. Movements are the production of change, such that each movement is already a change in everything else that moves. The movement-images of cinema are therefore neither the movements that merely realized pre-given eternal forms, nor movements that at any of their points are equivalent to all other points. It is by bringing dynamism to movements themselves that cinema takes a step beyond modern mechanism. While both modern science and cinema consider movement in terms of 'any-instant-whatever' (and no longer as the pre-modern notion of movement as the realization of a final pose) cinema connects images of movements that are productive of changes in the whole. This is what Deleuze takes to be the modern dialectic of Eistenstein: one captures a local, singular, seemingly unremarkable movement, or a 'privileged instant', and then cuts to the image of an altered social whole or moving mass of bodies. The key point is in seizing upon an instant that is not exemplary – just like any other – but *singular*: capable of changing the trajectory and relations of all instants. Bodies caught up in social movements do not perceive the smaller forces that add up to their actions; cinema gives us this supra-individual viewpoint by presenting images of potential change to the whole of life, not just changes for individuals. The capturing of movement-images therefore allows a cinematic author to *recompose* the production of the moving whole:

> The privileged instants of Eisenstein, or of any other director, are still any-instant-whatevers: to put it simply, the any-instant-whatever can be regular *or* singular, ordinary *or* remarkable. If Eisenstein picks out remarkable instants, this does not prevent him from deriving from them an immanent analysis of movement, and not a transcendental synthesis.[14]

A transcendental synthesis would refer movement back to some origin, such as the inevitable progress of history or humanity, whereas *immanent* analysis studies movements for themselves, the very potentials of movements to create history or humanity. It is not just that cinema captures movements or changes. In the technique of montage, where one movement is set against another movement – the movement of a factory cog or tractor, then the movement of a rebelling mass of people – one does not see time as that which sets one movement *after* another. Rather, movements are changes in the whole; time is no longer a series of equivalent moments, but a changing whole.

We can go back to Bergson's thesis on time and duration to give this distinction force. In order for the body or sensory-motor apparatus to make its way through the world, it perceives the world as an extended space, the same throughout time, thereby reducing change and locating movement within space. This *extended* space is '*relaxed*' because its points do *not* bear a relation to each other; the points are spread out and indifferent to each other. Euclidean geometry is a simple example of extended space; a plane can be divided into various sections, but the division of one section does not alter the character of another. In intensive space, however, an alteration of one point changes the quality of the whole. Indeed, intensive space is not made up of equivalent points; so, to add yet one more molecule, or one more degree of curvature, or one more degree of heat to an intensive quantity can change just what that quantity *is*. There are singularities or thresholds beyond which a quantity changes its identity and behaviour, so if we raise the temperature of this water by just one more degree it becomes steam. This distinction between extensive or relaxed space, and intensive and contracted space also has experiential implications. For the most part we do treat our lives as extended and relaxed: we look ahead in our diaries, planning one event after another. But it may, of course, happen that one event might preclude us from simply continuing our lives as we are. We meet our analyst every Wednesday at 11 a.m., but one week the session is so traumatic that I am altered; no appointment after that day is the same. The 'contracted' and enduring present of an experiencing subject regards the points that are other than itself from its own potentials, with each point changing in its potential according to the subject's ongoing life and from the point of view of what it might do: not everything is given. Intensive quantities such as an individual's life harbour singularities, or points that would alter the whole if change or movement were to occur.[15] We might have a degenerative eye disorder that gradually robs us of sight; for the first few years I move, think and live the world in the same way. But at a certain point my eyesight falls to a point where I have to adapt my movements, feel and think differently; and from then on each progressive fall in vision creates ever more intense changes.

Cinema gives images of movements that are genuine becomings through its *intensification* of singular points. An image bears a potential to alter what is not itself; it is not just an image of 'a' movement, but an image of the moving whole as expressed in this single movement. Human perception has the tendency to grasp 'immobile sections of movement'. This would occur if we saw a living, galloping, breathing, ageing horse as simply and reductively as 'a horse'. By contrast, cinema yields 'movement images which are *mobile* sections of duration'.[16] We see that this animal *is* its movements; we only know stable forms – such as the general concept of 'horse' – because we have discerned a relatively stable style of movement or a 'block of becoming.' The movement of the animal, machine or body is more than the movement of something that remains the same and *then* moves (or has movement simply added to it as a predicate). In the movement-image the movement is presented as definitive, essential or productive of that which, subsequently, we will fix into an immobile form. This is why cinema in its essence needs to be contrasted with cliché. At its worst, advertising presents movements in inevitable, automatic and pre-given relations: the desired object is seen to *cause* prestige, gratification or happiness in a general, necessary and global manner. Cinema, by contrast, has the power to present the contingent connections and relations among images. The whole is not given in advance; relations are effected from movements. In the cinema of the movement-image we are given an image of the synthesis, connection or movement of images. This is an indirect image of time, because time as duration, or as qualitative change, is beginning to be intuited. But this is not yet a direct image of time; for we are still seeing change as what happens from one movement to another, not change, duration or time itself.

How could we have an image of *time itself*? This problem exposes the audacity and originality of Deleuze's thought and goes beyond his arguments about cinema to the very nature of life: far from being committed to a notion that we only know life as it is mediated through knowledge and representation Deleuze remains committed to a radical metaphysical intuition, which cinema will both enable and betray (when cinema becomes clichéd or when we fail to think its potential). The betrayal can be warded off if we consider cinema alongside other powers of thought, including philosophy and the other arts. Cinema is not one more way of *representing* content from the human point of view; it is evidence that life gives itself to be thought in various styles.

THE WHOLE OF MOVEMENT

It is here that Deleuze's metaphysics – his argument that life is a changing multiplicity[17] of becomings – not a being that becomes but the potential for any movement or becoming to alter or connect with any other – is read from the physics of the cinema. Various techniques in cinema frame a set of movements, then cut with another set of movements, with the narrative of the film being produced from the composed sequences. In the case of both Eisenstein and D. W. Griffith, Deleuze looks at the way different cinematic techniques, different styles of framing and connection, produce different styles or wholes. That is, if one set of filmed movements cuts to another set, we can see how movements of nature – bodies and soil, farms and production – connect with social movements – acts of resistance, fatigue or abandonment. This produces a dialectic, where the whole is not a set of relations or laws *within* which contingent life unfolds; the whole is effected or created from the relations among images. The sets of images, in their very connection, yield an open whole, an 'indirect' or 'out-of-field':

The correlation between a non-human matter and a superhuman eye is the dialectic itself, because it is also the identity of a community of matter and a communism of man. And montage itself constantly adapts the transformation of movements in the material universe to the internal movement in the eye of the camera: rhythm.[18]

At the local level we could see a relative out-of-field – the revolution, social change or American dream – towards which connected movements contribute, as well as an open whole as such: alteration itself, that which differs and which allows any specified totality to take shape. There is a totality of movement which the camera happens not to take in (the relative out-of-field) and the totality that is not given, can never be given.[19] This open totality is the idea of time: time opens any movement to potentials that have not already taken place, and it is this power of time which is given relatively in the local out-of-field. There can only be the perception of *this* evolving history, the becoming of *this* people, nation or nature, if there is a power – time – for movements to produce a transformation beyond their immediate and adjacent connections. We can imagine the camera taking in more and more movements that all stand in relation to the American dream, but the camera cannot display the invisible principle of movement. The camera can only give this principle in what is not 'pragmatic', not given as part of the action or narrative, but indicated as a sense of change or alteration as such:

> In itself, or as such, the out-of-field already has two qualitatively different aspects: a relative aspect by means of which a closed system refers in space to a set which is not seen, and which can in turn be seen, even if this gives rise to a new unseen set, on to infinity; and an absolute aspect by which the closed system opens on to a duration which is immanent to the whole universe, which is no longer a set and does not belong to the order of the visible. Deframings which are not 'pragmatically' justified refer precisely to this second aspect as their raison d'être. In once case, the out-of-field designates that which exists elsewhere, to one side or around; in the other case, the out-of-field testifies to a more disturbing presence, one which cannot even be said to exist, but rather to 'insist' or 'subsist', a more radical Elsewhere, outside homogeneous space and time.[20]

This 'radical Elsewhere' opens from the non-pragmatic – movements or changes not oriented by an interested body or acting centre within the narrative. And this reinforces Deleuze's insistent subordination of narrative. We do not have a moving, changing scene of images in order to fulfil a narrative or order, to arrive at a point that is desired or anticipated in the beginning. On the contrary, there is narrative or the alteration of a situation because of the potential movements, which hold the real force and art of cinema. Throughout Deleuze's analysis of cinema he charts and affirms the non-narrative dimension and power of cinema. If narrative subordinates becoming and image to the fulfilment and realization of change *towards* some resolution, movement and change *itself* will free the perceiving eye and brain from the habits and genres of narrative, opening perception to a duration whose end is not given in advance. If this non-narrativity is possible, it is because Deleuze regards the signs of cinema *not* as components in a structure, but as productive of relations.

At a general level, Deleuze compares different schools – the Soviet schools, the post-war French school, the American school – showing how different formal techniques yield different styles of thought, and different ways of composing the whole. This formalism connects with Deleuze's more general claims in his other works regarding national styles and peoples. It is not that there are nations who then express identities – using their language to re-present what they already are in essence; rather, certain styles of enunciation (or in the case of cinema, construction) produce relatively stable collective bodies. A minor literature, or 'becoming-minoritarian', is a maximization of this essence of style.[21] When style is varied so that it produces new relations in an unheard-of manner then we see style in its creation and potential.[22] If style is presented as that which adequately captures an already given and stable set of relations, then style is enslaved to a majority. Hollywood cinema, with its formulae, sequels and remakes, is not only recognizable as a *way* of making films or as an attitude; it is directly recognizable in its repetition of effects. Indeed, it can take the productions of new styles and alternative cinema and return them to Hollywood form (such as when new cinema successes like *Nueve Reinas* (2000) or *Entre Tinieblas* (1983) issue in anodyne Hollywood versions such as *Criminal* (2004) or *Sister Act* (1992). Often romance plots or marriage narratives are injected in order to render the original minor or deviant film – the original attempt at mutation – into a readily consumable form.

Deleuze's taxonomy of the film schools of classical cinema is not the recognition of a series of themes or products, but the recognition of a repetition; each film fully repeats with all the force of the first time, the creative energy that opened a style. If Hollywood cinema creates once and then fails to take up that force of creation again, it offers us the image of a majoritarian cinema; all becoming or change is change *within* a set of norms and laws that govern alteration.

By contrast, Deleuze's national styles and schools, as examined in *Cinema 1*, are styles of variation. If the Soviet school works by connecting movements with an organic social whole, the French school allows for a cinematic sublime. In the case of the sublime, the whole opened up by images cannot be intuited or conceptualized but only felt; the material movements do not refer to a social organism (as in the Soviet school, where the totality is given the form of history, or in the American school where the totality is the 'American dream'); a feeling is given of the 'measureless spirit' only because the images connect towards the formation of a whole, for which no direct image is given.[23] Here Deleuze shows the ways in which the *metaphysical* idea of the sublime, with a philosophical and conceptual history going back to Kant and beyond, is given concretely in a specific technique of cinema and a style of image: local movements, or time as an interval between two changes, are contrasted with time as a whole, a historical immensity that is not given. Deleuze cites Abel Gance's *Napoléon* (1927), where the smallness of depicted detail contrasts with a historical becoming incapable of being fully comprehended.[24]

IMAGE AND LIFE

Both of Deleuze's volumes on cinema are dominated and led by local examples, where he demonstrates the construction of cinematic ideas from quite specific and formally defined uses of image. Not only does he look at various schools of cinema and their composition of images, he also looks at varieties within the movement image. This analytic practice forms part of a broader thesis regarding not merely perception and images, but the very nature of life. Deleuze can therefore be contrasted with a certain popular idea of what counts as postmodernism: that we only know the world or life as it is given through images, or that postmodernism is a movement that has abandoned knowledge, reality or any reference to life.[25]

Such a 'theory' presupposes that there is life on the one hand and then its simulation in images, even if this life is irrevocably lost or imaginary. Images, for Deleuze, are not images *of* life, such that there would be a life, in itself, that then had to be perceived or thought. Thought is, in one sense, life itself. Life is a dynamic and open whole, never fully given because it is always creating new connections and new potentials for further connection. Life is not composed of elements which *then* move or change; rather, there are movements and durations which are productive of relatively stable 'blocs of becoming'. The human eye is one enduring mobile section of becoming, with its potential altering as it encounters various other powers for change, each of its perceptions and movements altering, and altered by, all the other movements of life. This gives us a theory of life *as image*. There are not things – such as eyes and rays of light – which exist in themselves and then have to establish relations to each other (nor is the world already a set of stable relations, allowing things to enter into lawful and regular conjunctions). Rather, if we accept that life is composed from fluxes of change – light being a pulsation of vibrations perceived *as light* only when it encounters the eye, and the eye being a slower but no less enduring series of changes in cells and movements, which becomes *an eye* only when activated as a power to see – then we redefine the image radically. 'Image' is the power for something to be perceived; and perception and imaging go well beyond their human form to define relationality as such: something becomes what it *is*, only in its encounter with something else, its imaging or perception of another potential, another image: 'Even when they are nonliving, or rather inorganic, things have a lived experience because they are perceptions and affections.'[26] The human brain, on this account, is an image – not because it is a picture or figure we use to imagine the seat of thought but because the brain is a power to receive pulsations of becoming (light, sound, thought) from other images:

> We find ourselves in fact faced with the exposition of a world where IMAGE = MOVEMENT. Let us call the set of what appears 'Image'. We cannot even say that one image acts on another or reacts to another. There is no moving body [*mobile*] which is distinct from executed movement. There is nothing moved which is distinct from the received movement. Every thing, that is to say every image, is indistinguishable from its actions and reactions.

My eye, my brain, are images, parts of my body. How could my brain contain images since it is one image among others?[27]

If we accept this ontology – that there are not things that perceive each other and *then* move, but a universal variation of imaging from which one movement (such as the brain) reacts *in a certain way* to other movements (such as the cinema screen) – then we can begin to think philosophy anew. There can be no central immobile image, such as the brain or reason, from which all others unfold. Rather, we need to look at the production of images, from the image of thought to the images of bodies, without the appeal to a privileged image. The cinema books therefore look at imaging and perception *in general* (and then at how cinema extends these possibilities).

Deleuze outlines three possible movements between the perception and the image: subtraction, action and affect. In the subtractive perception image, the body perceives only those images that serve its purpose; we do not perceive the full temporal complexity of a scene but regard it as a set of relatively stable objects to be mastered. We do not simply act or react in full response to what we encounter but acknowledge only that which will concern us: 'When the universe of movement-images is related to one of these special images which forms a centre in it, the universe is incurved and organised to surround it.'[28] It is this subtraction, or possibility of *not* moving immediately to all we encounter, that allows for the action-image; here, we regard a set of images as a situation capable of transformation, and thereby open up a time mapped according to what is possible *for me.* The self is just this possibility for *decided* (or non-immediate) action:

> . . . perceiving things here where they are, I grasp the 'virtual action' that they have on me, and simultaneously the 'possible action' that I have on them, by diminishing or increasing the distance. It is thus the same phenomenon of the gap which is expressed in terms of space in my action and in terms of space in my perception.[29]

Deleuze argues that our grammar – nouns and verbs – is an expression of this orientation: perception subtracts from complexity to produce things/nouns, while perceiving what may be done allows for actions/verbs. In between the perception that subtracts from complexity to allow for action, but before the receptive brain–body moves in response, there is *affect*. Affect is not the thing itself, for we only have things insofar as we (as sets of movements) are respondents to other movements (the aural, visual and tactile vibrations of the world). Thus affect is just that vibratory or felt movement that may or may not result in action. Think, for example, of a missile hurtling towards me which I see and which I then act to deflect. Prior to action, we can think of all the changes in the body – the anxiety, tensing of muscles, flinching and alertness. If I do *not* act there would be, in addition to these imperceptible affects, the quite explicit affect or encounter of the pain as my body absorbs the impact of the missile. There are also more complex cases of affect where action is never actualized and where affect remains at the level of the virtual. An eye might encounter an image of another body, perceived as foreign, and *act* by thinking 'Who are all these people invading my space? We ought to be more strict with immigration; I must write to my MP.' But it is also possible, and common, for the body–eye–brain *not* to act, not to have the responding thought, but merely to feel the affect of loathing–fear–anxiety. In such cases it is not '*I*' who feels, for there is no decision or conscious relation to the encountered in terms of what I might or might not do. It is the acting self that creates a subject–object relation; the affective self *is* its encounters: 'There is inevitably a part of external movements that we "absorb", that we refract, and which does not transform itself into either objects of perception or acts of the subject; rather they mark the coincidence of the subject and the object in a pure quality.'[30] We need to note three key points here. First, there is a level of perception – or relation among bodies – that is not that of a subject grasping an object, but of a vibration or merging. My eye–body–brain feels the image, responding viscerally, but does not yet adopt or decide what it/I *will do*. Second, affect is prior or primary (but not in a standard idea of time as simply coming before). In order for there to be a self *that* decides or pictures its world there has to be some differentiation, and this is established through affect. If the body were to respond immediately to encounters – to eat when hungry, drink when thirsty, retreat when an excess of stimulus intrudes – then it would be pure perception, nothing more than what is caused by an outside.[31] It is only in *not* acting, in *not* expending energy but in 'absorbing' the force of the image, that something like a site of pooled energy as the reception of affect can be formed. If we return to the example of pain: in not eating, or not deflecting a hurtling missile, there is a feeling of hunger or pain, with the self being built up from such affective receptions. Third, this primacy of affect allows for a politics and ethics (as well as a theory of cinema and image) that is pre-personal. We tend to think of politics primarily as ideology – the thoughts, ideas or attitudes from which we act and move; but the acting moving self is produced, Deleuze and Guattari argue, *from affect*. At the simplest level, it is only after the delay of affect, the capacity for what is other than the self to produce a vibration or received movement in the body, that there can be a self who results from this 'zone' of feeling, of *not* acting – the zone of indetermination.

Deleuze's (and Deleuze and Guattari's) politics of affect has its source in the *autonomy* of affect.[32] We can have a politics that attends to the explicit pronouncements and actions among bodies, but we also need a *micropolitics*, which attends to the passional connections among bodies – the way certain images, ranging from whiteness to the fascist leader, are charged with an erotic responsive energy. The psychoanalytic idea of investment as it functions in Deleuze and Guattari's *Anti-Oedipus* relies on such a recognition of affect. Investment describes a flow of energy that does not expend itself in action but is *cathected* or circuited on an external body; the energy that would expend itself in hunger, for example, may allow the breast to captivate and halt action, producing a surface or virtual layer of fantasy. The virtual objects that dominate life begin, not from an action tied to the immediate need of life or the sensory-motor apparatus, but from a certain delay. In not acting and in allowing the other body's force to resonate in my own, 'I' am produced as a zone of indetermination, not caused or immediately responding to forces outside me, but creating a new layer of relations. In *not* eating but imagining an object of desire a relation is produced to a virtual object, with the self being nothing more than a regularity or cathexis of objects, and with social assemblages being nothing more than relations or territories oriented to privileged, invested or affective images. We can even see contemporary nationalism not as the way a body of people consciously defines itself, but as a pool of affects or partial objects – such as the Union Jack, the royal family, Premier League football, the Tate Modern. It is the desiring perception of such invested images that produces relations among perceiving bodies. We can see this quite clearly in cases of collective spectacle, such as the announcement of the staging of the 2012 Olympics. Images of this announcement, and images of jubilant response, were relayed repeatedly throughout the media on 6 July 2005; the next day contrasting images of grief, shock and horror were relayed following the terrorist attacks on the London underground. A collective body is produced through such images, which have both a direct affect, and then a reflective affect as we see the workings of these images on others. Cameras typically film a group of observers receiving the news, producing affecting images of affected bodies. Being British is effected from the power of images to produce affect, with affect thereby producing bodies as a collective. Before there can be riotous or collective action – the exercise of power – there have to be the productive desires which assemble the bodies collectively, creating a territory. Once affect or the *non-actualization* of energy creates its own relations or surfaces it is then possible that the deferred action – the non-expenditure of energy that allowed an object to be invested or maintain a certain force – might re-orient action. The supposedly natural action grounded in immediate life is delayed in affect; we do not satisfy hunger immediately but establish a desiring relation to the possible object of satisfaction; this virtual object then creates a self that is *not* life in an immediate and fully given actuality, but is a potential for action, a relation to an object that is not cognitive or representative but desiring.

BECOMING INHUMAN, BECOMING IMPERCEPTIBLE

The three orders of image – the action-image, perception-image and (in between those two) the affection-image – describe the emergence of the subject from relations of movement, action/reaction and delay. This structure leads Deleuze to formulate a problem: 'How can we rid ourselves of ourselves, and demolish ourselves?'[33] To a great extent Deleuze sees this is the problem of cinema. Already, in the dialectical montage of Eisenstein, the human body is freed from its personal locale; the cuts in images refer to broader movements, such as those of history, nations or nature. But it is also this problem – the problem of overcoming the human, of becoming imperceptible – which carries cinema beyond the movement-image. For while the movement-image gives us an *indirect* image of time – that is, it combines local movements with an open moving whole – it nevertheless gives that whole a specific scene: a history, a national consciousness, even a nature so immense as to be glimpsed only through its effects. Deleuze details the ways in which classical cinema broadens the perception-image (of things), the action-image (of verbs) and the affection-image (of qualities) away from the human observer. The perception-image is no longer this horizon or set of images for me, centred in this point in time and space; nor is it universalized to become timeless and abstract. Geometry, for example, perceives in the space of the here and now what is true for all space, and thereby abstracts from any possible observer. Cinema is not abstraction but subtraction. The actions and interests that would fold the scene around 'me' are removed. The camera's eye functions to give a style of scene that is at once that of an observer, but is not personal. The camera 'sees' the scene: in a certain way, but not from the point of view of a character. Deleuze cites the example of Dziga Vertov's (1896–1954) montage, where 'Everything is at the service of variation and interaction: slow on high speed shots, superimposition, frag-mentation, deceleration [*démultiplication*], micro-shooting [*micro-prise de vue*]. This is not a human eye – even an improved one.'[34]

In the case of the action-image the situation for which movement is possible is no longer oriented to a local, personal agent but is expanded to milieus, so that action is not that of a body responding to a stimulus, but concerns a larger domain of multiple interacting movements. In the Western, for example, the encounter of a hero with an adversary takes place in a scene that broadens the action to the social body and environment. Deleuze looks at the way American cinema uses images to open action on to milieus: no longer is the body acting against an object, for images of the sky, the open country, and the town expose any movement to a multiplicity of other movements. Movement is no longer the movement *from* some fixed point of view – the movement of things within an extended space – but one moving life, a whole composed of movements of different speeds. This reading of relations, and what counts as a pos-sible movement, derives from the concrete element of cinematic images. Deleuze therefore regards the cinematic technology as expos-ing a potential of life. If the human eye only sees movement in rela-tion to its own centre, the cinematic eye can open on to movements no longer folded around the bodily observer. In the films of John Ford (1894–1973) and Howard Hawks (1896–1977), for example, a shot of the sky can open relations among images:

> Encompassed by the sky, the milieu in turn encompasses the col-lectivity. It is as representative of the collectivity that the hero becomes capable of an action which makes him equal to the

milieu and re-establishes its accidentally or periodically endangered order: mediations of the community and of the *land* are necessary in order to form a leader and render an individual capable of such a great action.[35]

Finally, the affection-image (the pause or delay which is neither a subject seeing an object, nor an action transforming a situation, but an absorption of movement by an inactive but receptive body) has its cinematic liberation in 'any-space-whatever'. One no longer sees this city or building, in this historical, narrative moment, nor this event as part of a series for a collective of bodies, but perceives a power as such, a power to be seen, an extended quality that is not located in *this* space but is 'a' space. As an example, Deleuze looks forward to the modern colourism of Jean-Luc Godard, where colours are not signs of qualities – green for jealousy – nor are colours ways of grasping objects – where the colour would be the colour *of* this identifiable thing. Colours become pure affects through which objects might be perceived or feelings might be expressed, but which have a potential above and beyond reference, the pure potential of colour:

> In opposition to a simply coloured image, the colour-image does not refer to a particular object, but absorbs all that it can: it is the power which seizes all that happens within its range, or the quality common to completely different objects . . . Colour is . . . the affect itself, that is, the virtual conjunction of all the objects which it picks up.[36]

We can note here that the affection-image in cinema brings in the virtual, or what Deleuze refers to earlier in *Cinema 1* (discussing Bresson) as the spiritual. The virtual is implicit in Deleuze's discussion of the image, but comes increasingly to the fore as he details the perception-image, action-image and affection-image; for these images are sorted according to their unfolding of a relation between actual and virtual. At its 'purest' perception would be fully actual; eye and image would coincide, there would be no *idea of*, or perception *of*, what is imaged. There would be nothing other than the meeting point of eye and light. But such a non-relational, immediate and full image is not what we usually understand by perception (and the whole point of Deleuze's emphasis on life as imaging is that we are always dealing with perceptions that are relational, directed with some anticipation or virtual surplus). Pure perception is an ideal limit, with perception generally already being on its way towards the action-image. In the perception-image when I see things as they are for me I am already anticipating or 'curving' the situation around myself, subtracting from the fullness of vibrations but also opening and adding the possibility or anticipation of action. The action-image brings the virtual to the fore; what I perceive is not just what is actually present, but also what I might do, what might happen: I act on this scene with a sense of who I am (my virtual moral or social self, the image I have of myself). In the affection-image, when action does *not* take place, the vibrations or movements have not produced actual relations – a body that acts – but powers to act. If action-images are those of milieus – scenes of interaction and movement among bodies – affection-images are those of *singularities*, powers that potentially yield relations not already given.[37] In the case of colour, the redness is the colour that one sees, could see, and that could have been seen not only here and now but in any space whatever. One perceives the power to be perceived as such, the virtual power of colour: not colour as it is perceived here and now (perception-image), nor colour as it is for me and my meaningful world (action-image), but colour's power to be perceived. By working with affection-images cinema liberates the relations among images beyond movement – beyond relations between and among terms – and opens the thought of time: not things that move, but the power of alteration or difference that is expressed in movement. In order to understand this we need to follow Deleuze's deduction of the movement image. That is, if we ask *how* a movement-image works we will see that it already brings in the virtual and that the true nature of the virtual is not the possible (what one can or cannot do in this space) but the potential: the power to differ or become, change itself, and not that which changes. This pure potentiality, liberated from the potential *of* this or that imaged thing, is time.

THE DEDUCTION OF THE MOVEMENT-IMAGE

Deleuze's emphasis on deduction has a twofold significance. First, it is in keeping with his overall transcendental philosophical commitment. One should never simply accept a constituted order or set of relations as given but should ask what movements gave birth to those relations. How did the three orders of movement-image – perception, action and affection – emerge? Second, this transcendental insistence both reinforces the importance of cinema (for cinema itself works through this problem of the logic of images) and allows us to think beyond cinema. There is a broader problem at work in Deleuze's cinema books: if perception has a history and that history is also a logic of life – the tendency for the brain to form an image of itself as an acting centre in an immobilized scene – then cinema may offer one opening on to the virtual (or all those powers and potentials that the sensory-motor apparatus of the human body has *not* brought to presence). The virtual is *the* problem of life. There is no question of the human eye ever having only the actual before it – just those present objects here and now for me and nothing more (for the very notion of 'object' and 'me' has already perceived the world in a certain style and for a certain anticipated end) – but the virtual or potentially perceivable is reduced to an image of the actual. We imagine or think of the virtual only as what is *not* actualized, as parasitic on the actual. We think of the virtual as possibilities added on to the scene before us, whereas the scene before us is a diminution of the virtual, *one* of the ways life might be perceived or actualized. The notion of 'virtual reality' today is evidence of this tendency, whereby we think of the virtual as something creatively added on to, or simulating, an actual world (where only the actual is fully real). For Deleuze, however, the virtual is real and it is only because of virtual potentials that the actual extended world is realized, cut out from a virtual multiplicity of connections and variations. If we could think the virtual from itself, in and for itself, we would think worlds and futures beyond the habits, clichés and banalities of this located and personal body. But what is the virtual for itself? To understand this we need to see the genesis of the movement-image, and its dependence on the virtuality it then enslaves.

FIRSTNESS One of the most remarkable features of Deleuze's thought is his anti-linguisticism, evidenced most fully in his tirades against the 'despotism of the signifier' in *A Thousand Plateaus*. Whereas structuralist semiotics in its simple and widely disseminated forms insists that there are no positive terms, and that one is always already located within a system of relations, Deleuze makes two key departures. To begin with, he repeatedly argues that relations are external to terms; that is, there are *no* pre-given or a priori systems or structures through which the world is given, no single structure that would determine relations, differences or differentiation in advance. The idea that the world is constructed through a language or conceptual scheme is rejected by Deleuze, and for sound metaphysical reasons. If there were some system, law or structure of categories through which the world were ordered, how would we account for that which is ordered? We would have to posit something, some substance, which is structured. So the system of relations or structure would then have to relate to this substance that it structures; there would always be one more relation, and the structure itself would be one more relating term. Concretely, if we were to see the world as 'socially constructed' through language, culture or concepts, we could then ask who or what is doing the structuring, and who or what is structured. No structure or set of relations can be closed, can account for relationality is such. Instead of arguing for a set of relations or structure that determines life and difference in advance, Deleuze looks at the production of relations. Experience or perception is not structured in advance; rather, each event of experience is productive of relations that are genuinely new, that could not have been predicted on the basis of an already given principle.

This emphasis on relations is related to Deleuze's second truly post-structuralist manoeuvre. Following the semiotics of C. S. Peirce, Deleuze insists upon *firstness*. Generally, in our actual world, we only have to do with secondness and thirdness. Secondness is the domain of relations: the light that assails my eye, the heat that melts the ice, the body that is fuelled by food – all these actions and reactions produce a world or space of terms and individuals. Firstness is the potential or power *to relate*: that which has not yet been realized or actualized in any relation, but is a pure power or quality – in itself and singular. However, firstness, according to Peirce, is nevertheless a level of sign, for a sign can be read and is open to a possible response. This means that there is not a world *and* then some way of signifying a reality that exists in itself; the world is already signifying, a potential to produce relations, perceptions and interpretations; firstness is first only in the production of secondness and thirdness. Deleuze will therefore use the word 'sign' as he uses the words 'image' and 'perception'; we have actual systems of signs, images and perceptions but these do not double a world that is self-present and radically prior to relations, for the world just 'is' its imaging, perceiving or 'signing'. When we read the signs of secondness we consider an actualized relation; the light that meets the eye is perceived as colour; the heat that melts the ice is observable as a sign of nature's ecosystem; the body fuelled by energy is lived as a sense of satiation or well-being. Thirdness is this 'reading' or interpretant of secondness. Thirdness, for Peirce, extends indefinitely. For we can always take a thirdness that has related two terms and relate this to another term, producing a new third. If, for example, the light that meets the eye is perceived as colour, but that colour is read as a blush signifying embarrassment, and that embarrassment is then read as a sign of a social *faux pas*, and that social *faux pas* is then read (say, in a Jane Austen novel) as a sign of civility in general, then the relations are still triadic: the initial relation – colour – meets with another term to produce another relation, for the colour read as a blush must meet with the idea of emotion to be read as embarrassment. Now Deleuze will disagree with Peirce's claim that all we ever achieve is thirdness. (This has to do with his departure from Peirce's pragmatism. For Peirce we know that there must be, *must have been*, something like firstness which offers itself to be read; but all we can do is continually reinterpret and rework our relations to firstness, never establish an overarching law for our interpretation of relations, nor can we get beyond relationality itself.)

Deleuze's primary difference from Peirce is to tie firstness to *expression*. Firstness is expression, which means that there is not a who or what that expresses, but expressions – pulsations of difference or powers, *from which* one might posit a thing that is given in expression. This thing or result of expression would be secondess, and our perception of the secondness would be thirdness. Light is expression; light that meets the eye produces a relation; that relation perceived as this identifiable and repeatable shade of red is thirdness. Whereas firstness in Peirce has a predominantly heuristic value, Deleuze insists not only that we ought to strive to overcome the actual world as it is constituted in relation to us, but also that cinema and the affection-image can give us the experience of pure qualities. Peirce, in his philosophy of science, was aware that we know the world through relations, and that science not only must constantly work towards agreement among observers, but must also be open to those powers that elicit relations, the potentials that produce experience (firstness). Deleuze's affection-images may be part of a cinematic science, and may be read as signs of something other than their immediate power; they open the way towards the thought of 'pure affections'.[38]

If cinema generally helps us work back from constituted spaces and fields of centred experience to their genesis, then the affection-image is crucial as a sign of the powers which, though actualized in this particular way here, are also powers to be actualized in further and other relations:

> The affect is independent of all determinate space-time; but it is none the less created in a history which produces it as the expressed and the expression of a space or a time, of an epoch or a milieu (this is why the affect is the 'new' and new affects are ceaselessly created notably by the work of art).[39]

AFFECT How does art create affects? The opening to affect lies in the liberation from milieu, so that art does not see this red as mere paint on a canvas – the actual. Nor does one interpret this red as a sign of some other actuality – the mood of the artist – by relating the colour to social convention. Rather, in art one confronts a singular power, which entails *dissolving oneself as an observer*: the red should not be seen in relation to me, but as a power to be seen. The affect would then no longer be located in this observational space. It would become a power to express itself, not just in this here and now but for all time. Art's powers are tied to the event; there is in life, as pure and real potential, a power for all that will and can happen. It is this presence of events – not only what has happened but the reality of all time, the eternity of events – that is opened by art:

> [P]ower-qualities have an anticipatory role, since they prepare for the event which will be actualized in the state of things and will modify it (the slash of the knife, the fall over the precipice). But in themselves, or as expressed, they are already the event in its eternal aspect.[40]

Affects are not actions (or powers exerted) but *powers to*. Is not cinema the power to *feel* fear, desire, tragedy or melancholy without oneself being afraid, desirous, afflicted or depressed? The power or affect itself is given, in itself, not as it is actualized in lives. On the one hand, then, the power-qualities of art do refer to what is possible in our lives; but on the other hand they also bear an autonomy, for we can only become afraid or desirous because *there is* fear or desire. This is the eternal power to be afraid, to desire – not reducible to any of its instances. Deleuze cites the close-up in his account of affection-images as a passage to pure-qualities. At one level the close-up would seem to be a good example of thirdness: we see the face of Garbo and then respond to it as a sign of stardom or glamour. But this is not the real power of the close-up. As the camera moves in we depart from characters, narrative and relations; we do not see who or what is feared, nor *who* is afraid; the face becomes impersonal and one is given fear as such, the pure affect of fear:

> There is no close-up of the face. The close-up is the face, but the face precisely in so far as it has destroyed its triple function – a nudity of the face much greater than that of the body, an inhumanity much greater than that of animals.[41]

The fear could, therefore, be anybody's fear at any time whatever. In its singularity it is also therefore eternal and also truly different, for it is no longer grasped in terms of relations and generalities or as a quality of some underlying actuality, but as it is in itself, in its purity: 'The close-up has merely pushed the face to those regions where the principle of individuation ceases to hold sway.'[42] That is, the face becomes *singular* – not comparable to, or signifying, a generality – and therefore no longer an individual; it is not one face, one of a number, but 'a' face, a singular style that may be repeatable but is not an instance of what is already repeated.

One might say that there is a problem of knowing firstness. Indeed, given Deleuze's emphasis on relations, connections, desire and machines, there might appear to be a conflict between his emphasis on one immanent, connected and productive life on the one hand, and singularities or firstness on the other. But despite his insistence that relations are external to terms – that terms are effected from relations – Deleuze nevertheless insists on not reducing life to relations. So if relations do not exhaust life, how do we know or experience firstness or singularities? Knowledge is, by definition, already relational. If we are to know something then we must experience it, or receive it in some manner. Accordingly, the epistemological challenge of Deleuze's philosophy, with its emphasis on affect, firstness, intuiting the inhuman and overcoming the actual observational point of the here and now, is *how* (other than by imagining it as some sort of 'beyond') can we know firstness?

Deleuze's most vivid response comes in the cinema books, where the true experience of cinema is not cognitive, such that 'I' grasp the seen *as* this or that communicable, general and conceptual given. Rather, the camera's eye short-circuits the constituted, human and located point of view of perception, and does this by disrupting the habitual order of images that allows an 'I' point to relate to, and order, a stable world. Affection images go some way towards freeing the human eye from its organized milieu, where the seen is grasped by a deciding and organizing observer. One could only have an affection-image – or *not* see the face as this named person from this narrative, played by this actor – if the cinematic viewer has already been displaced from his or her position of knowledge and recognition. Affect is, generally, an aspect or part of experience; we experience the other's face in part as an object of knowledge (perception-image), in part as something that demands a response on our part (action-image) and in part as something that assails us (affection-image). Cinema can isolate or disclose affect by subduing our knowing and acting tendencies. This tendency towards the autonomy of affect applies to art in general, but the significance of cinema lies in the coupling of this tendency with a radically inhuman technology. A picture in a gallery or even the stained-glass image in a cathedral may well have been isolated from the world of functional action and knowledge, so that art in general is expressed in distinction from the world of habit, connections and work. But the power of art to stand alone, to be released from the human eye's tendency to synthesize its experiences into a world of its own, is given a stunning form in cinema. Once we can think of an image that is not the image *of* this located human observer, then all art can be understood not as expressions *of* humanity but as the release of imagination from its human and functional home. It is in this sense that the century of cinema has also been the century of non-narrative, non-representational and affective art. The most extreme example is surrealism, where art is not designed to produce pleasure or recognition but aims to disrupt the brain's cognitive and harmonizing powers to produce thought or experience that is not that of the organism, not one's own.

Deleuze does not just express a utopian vision of a cinema that would liberate thought from its mechanisms; he also deduces the movement-image. The notion of a deduction goes back to Kant; we cannot simply assert the 'beyond' of what is experienced, but we can move from what is actual or experienced to ask what life must be such that experience takes the form that it does. We can deduce the existence of the unconditioned from the conditioned world we experience; the process of deduction is therefore one of moving back from an experience to explain its possibility. Deleuze therefore asks how the movement-image is possible. How can we present an image of the movements from which milieus are constituted? If the eye grasps each pulsating, differing and enduring potential of life in terms of its own human point of view, reducing the flux of life to a set of things, it can also retrace this actualized world and think the movements or affects from which relatively stable or immobilized sections have been cut. That is, we can move back from the actual world of things folded around our own point of view to intuit the virtual potentials from which the world has been unfolded. One way this can be done is through the movement-image and montage: by joining movements that are not usually connected we can disrupt the habits of vision, and in so doing we get a sense of the connective or synthesizing process. We can indirectly refer to the whole of a moving historical life. This could occur when montage presents the movements that are not connected by the human eye, but rely for their synthesis on filmic cuts. One relatively recent example would be Patrick Keiller's *London* (1994) that creates a political archaeology of the city. Scenes alternate between pictures of striking workers, jubilant election victory scenes, and then falling and . rising stock-markets. Movement is no longer the movement of a body across space, but is given as the image of a connecting whole, such that the movements of bodies produces the movements of markets and voters. We no longer view the world as movements from the point of a fixed and mastering eye, but become aware of movements not reducible to ordering humanity; humanity is located within movement and movement is freed from the movement *of things*. The power of movement as such is given in this image of interconnected actions and reactions that are not grounded on, for example, a humanity or nation that *then* moves. London is given as a series of layered and moving connections; it has no existence outside the movements that make up its relative stability. This provides one way to understand the thinking of firstness. London, like any city, is produced by relations among potentials; bodies, machines, spaces and rhythms connect to form regular movements such that an identity is established through time. By presenting images of these connecting movements – abstracting from the eye of any located observer to shift from markets to bodies to the formation of a political body – movement is given as the power of change, not the change from position to position, but the altering whole of life.

Peirce's semiotics arrives at firstness, or potentials, by moving back from thirdness: we are always in a world where we speak about and refer to relations. When we talk about any object we are giving an 'interpretation' of what is seen – a relation – and we could, in turn, interpret the way we view objects. Thirdness moves outwards infinitely for Peirce, and firstness or the power to produce images is always deduced or given from achieved thirdness or images. Deleuze marks two differences of his own approach from Peirce; he thinks that cinema can liberate us from relational and mediated thinking (always being within thirdness), and that there is a point then at which the notion of an image of an image of an image (or ever-expanding thirdness) can be halted. This would be when there is an image, not of this or that relation, but imaging as such, the power *to image*. What the movement-image has to do is not focus on an object which then moves, but somehow connect objects such that they are seen as resulting from movement. This would give us an indirect image of time, where time is the force *for difference* from which movements emerge. Another way to approach firstness or give an image of the potential for relations, would be to take the movement-image beyond itself. Life would no longer be posited as that which expressed itself in the different becomings or rhythms of movement, a life that would be given indirectly or inferred back from the connections of movements. Potentials or 'powers to become' would no longer be posited as conditions of the actual world; one would have an image of the differing power itself. If the perception of movement is initially possible only because the eye grasps the world from a point that stabilizes the flux of life into bodies that move, then the dislocation and disorientation of the eye may enable a perception of becoming as such. Deleuze arrives at this possibility by contesting the assumption that once we read the world as 'ours' – the thirdness of seeing relations from the point of view of an observer – all we can do is reinterpret (producing ever more complex critiques of our own point of view). Thirdness, he argues, provides a way to another dimension. Thirdness, on one level, is thought. My body is a power which encounters other powers, (such as other bodies with which I might struggle); but if I consider this struggle as it might be for another, or if I take an image of my body's relation to its world, the reactions of my body are recorded or *doubled* in thought. Deleuze argues that we *act* not when our bodies respond habitually but when we have an image of our body's relations. With thirdness, or our capacity to *think* of relations and not just be caught up in relations, we open up relations of desire. I do not just *react* to what is actual; I *act* or move my body in accord with affects that I might *imagine* or *anticipate*. Desire would be just this perception of a not-yet, a power or potential for virtual relations added to already actualized relations. If I *act*, as opposed to simply reacting, then one might say that I do so for a reason; I anticipate or imagine the general power or predictable outcome of what I will do. Thirdness is effected when bodies move beyond action and reaction but become capable of *acting*, of relating to another power *for* some intended or imagined end, some further relation:

> Therefore, thirdness gives birth not to actions but to 'acts' which necessarily contain the symbolic element of a law (giving, exchanging), not to perceptions, but to interpretations which refer to the element of sense: not to affections but to intellectual feelings of relations, such as the feelings which accompany the use of the logical conjunctions 'because', 'although', 'so that', 'therefore', 'now', etc.[43]

In referring to thirdness as 'sense' Deleuze not only picks up on an important area of his earlier work (*The Logic of Sense*); he also opens a possible departure from the triadic strictness of Peirce, for whom we are always committed to argue from *within relations*. For Deleuze, the power of sense or thirdness can restrict thought. The relations established by common sense, the clichéd connections repeated in so much Hollywood cinema and 'unthinking thought', the system of signification which afflicts us with an 'interpretosis'[44] – the one system through which all other signs will be read: all these are examples of the ways in which a produced orientation or milieu of sense can close further connections. But the *potential* and power of sense or thirdness – the very fact that powers have produced not just relations with each other, but a further relation capable of reflecting upon or perceiving other relations – allows for the thought of relationality as such:

> . . . we have encountered signs which, eating away at the action-image, also brought their effect to bear above and below, on perception and relation, and called into question the movement-image

as a whole: these are opsigns or sonsigns. The interval of move-ment was no longer that in relation to which the movement-image was specified as perception-image, at one end of the interval, as action-image at the other end, and as affection-image between the two, so as to constitute a sensory-motor whole. On the contrary the sensory-motor link was broken, and the interval of move-ment produced the appearance as such of an image other than movement-image.[45]

This possibility of intuiting the virtual power of relations beyond constituted relations is brought to the fore in cinema. Cinema pro-duces a non-human eye, outside the actions/reactions of generalized responses of the practical body. It is this new point of view that allows for a perception of relations – or what Deleuze refers to as the thought-image.

In *Difference and Repetition* Deleuze sets his own philosophy against a history of philosophy that has begun from an 'image of thought'. Traditionally, relations have been derived from some sub-stance, such as the modern subject, who perceives the world in terms of correct categories. Plato, for example, argued that we view the world through pre-given and eternal forms or essences, while Kant argued that there were transcendental categories that give our experience a necessary order. According to Deleuze, the 'image of thought' has determined what counts as proper thinking – say, in terms of truth and error – and has failed to ask about the *genesis* of thought. How is it that the relations of the world, or life, produce something like the brain that can have an image of those relations? Sense, for Deleuze, is the milieu or capacity for relations, the orien-tation or map, within which thought moves;[46] in a very simple sense a basketball player does not just perceive the ball and then process this perception according to pre-given rules, for his entire body and way of thinking is oriented to his position on the court, the position of other players, the position of the net, and the temporal point of the game. Deleuze insists that this milieu of sense is what makes explicit language and concepts possible; we can only form a system or blueprint for doing *after* there have already been relations or con-nections. It is this *virtual* realm of sense which Deleuze draws upon to open up the rigid images of thought that have dominated philoso-phy. If Plato thinks of the mind as capable of turning away from sense experience to intuit the eternal forms that give order and truth to our perceptions, then this is because he has already assumed a set of relations and movements that would then make the act of proper thinking possible. For Deleuze the task of philosophy today is not to produce one more image of what counts as good thinking, but to create a concept of the *difference* from which various orientations of thinking emerge.

To approach 'thought without an image' would be one of the highest ideals of a philosophy of immanence which did not include the creativity of relations *within* some creating term (seeing immanence as immanence *to* some transcendent). The thought-image in cinema is not that of a thinking character, caught up in actions and passions; the thought-image is the purification of actual thoughts, presenting thought as such. Deleuze acknowledges that we never have firstness or secondness in pure form: affects already tend towards powers to act – there is always some minimal relation or response to the world we are given, and the produced actions already tend towards the thoughts that would make sense of them. What Deleuze strives to do, not only in his cinema books but throughout his work, is to intuit the essence of movement: not as movement from or towards that which remains the same (the movements of bodies in space), but as movement that creates a specific difference. In the thought-image, which may be set within affects and actions, we are presented with the power to think as such, what it is *to think*. We do not see a character looking puzzled or angry – thinking confusion or rage – but we are presented with thought affects, or what thought can do. As an example, Deleuze refers to Hitchcock and suspense. Instead of having bodies act and react immediately as they would do in a standard fight scene or duel, Hitchcock manages to halt the action so that the character is poised at the moment of being *about to act*. The potential *to act* is given an image: not what *is* or what a character would do (the actual), but what might be, or the potential actions from which any character is constructed. In Hitchcock, actions appear as what *will happen*; this is not just because of genre expectations (many of which were created by Hitchcock) but because of cuts in images that display both objects and persons as caught up in relations of action. Action and affection are liberated from the characters within the scene. Going beyond the interactions of bodies and the logic of the narrative we are also given a psychological scene, and we are given this *visually* – not through voice-overs or stated narrative. The knife on the table is threatening as such, presenting itself as that which will cut and kill; the knife is *what can be thought of as threatening* – 'a' threat. In the 'mental image' we see the thoughts that are not thoughts *of* a character: once again, cinema produces an image of the virtual. The mental image,

> . . . is an image which takes as objects of thought, objects which have their own existence outside thought, just as the objects of perception have their own existence outside perception. *It is an image which takes as its object, relations, symbolic acts, intellectual feelings.*[47]

In the thought-image one grasps the power of sense: the way produced relations exist as potentials for actions of bodies, actions that may or may not be actualized. We see the domain of sense: not just the interactions of bodies, but the way the assemblage of bodies might be viewed or made sense of – the scene as it is surveyed and assessed by a point of view, with characters being unfolded as a potential space of actions. There is a fold-back effect. There can only be actions/reactions if there are powers to act (firstness), and there can only be perception of relations if relations have been actualized (secondness); but the perception of relations *as relations* opens the scene such that we may *finally* think beyond the movements within which we are located. In a Hitchcock film, which vividly portrays the force of relations, we are given an image of thirdness – not just movements or tendencies to move, but systems or frames which hold those movements together:

> In Hitchcock, actions, affections, perceptions, all is interpretation from beginning to end . . . The reason for this is simple: in Hitchcock's films an action, once it is given (in present, future or past) is literally surrounded by a set of relations, which vary its subject, nature, aim etc. What matters is not who did the action – what Hitchcock calls with contempt the whodunit – but neither is it the action itself: it is the set of relations in which the action and the one who did it are caught. This is the source of the very special sense of the frame.[48]

Deleuze's philosophy of immanence therefore refuses to posit some superior term – such as mind – which explains thinking. Rather, his task is to begin with the power to think, and then the ways in which that power is actualized by minds. This means that he does not begin with an *actual* explanation – explaining mind biologically or from an evolutionary perspective, for such an explanation would always have to begin with one privileged image – such as the concept of biological life. By contrast, Deleuze begins with the virtual. We know that there are powers *to think*, and that this is a power for forming relations; biological life is also created from powers of forming relations. Virtual explanations are immanent because they do not assume a first term from which relations emerge.

In the first cinema book, Deleuze's example of Hitchcock as an author who presented an image of relations leads us up to the problem of the time-image. In cinema the time-image is opened through three paths: the time-crystal, peaks of present and sheets of past, and the powers of the false. The time-crystal presents the virtual alongside the actual: the peaks of present link a present image with its virtual past, and the powers of the false display the dissimulation that does not overlay some underlying real world, for the 'real' world *is* just all that appears and becomes.

FROM MOVEMENT-IMAGE TO TIME-IMAGE   There is both a problem and an opening in Deleuze's *Cinema 1* at this point. How do we go beyond the image of relations to the image of the virtual power from which relations emerge? Hitchcock's style of cinema might give us the form of reflecting and recursive relations – 'He sees that she sees, and sees that she sees him seeing, and in seeing him . . .' We see the way in which the perception of relations produces further relations; if I know that you know that I have a secret, this knowing of your knowing might become a further secret. If the thought-image presents relations *as such* rather than just operating through the manipulation of narrative elements, then we move close to the image or thought of the virtual.

Deleuze's history of cinema has a normative trajectory, with cinema moving progressively closer to the achievement of what it is most capable of doing. In the time-image, cinema will not be a copy of the human eye, nor a tracker of actual movements, but will create its own movements and its own time – the time, for example, in which something actual *and* the multiplicity of its potentials would be equally present. This would occur if we were given a character who was not a self played by or mimed by an actor, but a self who was nothing more than a series of acts. There would not be a real self who then takes on a role, but a self who is nothing outside of his appearances. We could distinguish, then, between 'imposter' films that present a character who *masks himself* – such as *The Talented Mr Ripley* (1999) where a character desires to be what he is not and wants to hide who he *really is* for reasons of external gain or psychological gratification – from 'dissimulator' films where there is no real self. In Christopher Nolan's *Memento* (2000) the central character played by Guy Pierce has no memory and is compelled to write marks on his own body and surrounding environment to keep track of the plot of his own life. Because he has no mind that is his own – for his *present* mind is composed of notes, tattoos, and other reminders – these external memory aids can be manipulated by others, and misinterpreted by his later 'new' self. His 'self' becomes a series of narratives that are partly self-inscribed, partly inscribed by others and partly mis-transcribed by himself after having been prompted or rewritten by others; he has no being or substance outside these inscriptions and copyings. What we get in this film is not an actual self who *then* takes on a virtual or fictional role, but a self whose very actuality of being *in the present* is virtual. His *actual* world of inscribed memories, characters who lie to him, and marks on his body, is the result of a copying of what never took place, a series of signs with no referent. This 'power of the false' is an image of the virtual: not an actual world that then goes through change, nor a self who then takes on a part, but a life or self that *is* only its differences, distortions and simulations.

When cinema (as in the thought-image of Hitchcock) 'makes relation itself the object of an image'[49] this is the cinematic counterpart of a philosopher who does not simply inhabit a system of signs or relations but asks *how relations emerge* (a transcendental philosopher). This yields two possibilities. The first is to posit, even if we cannot know or think it concretely, some substance or being from which relations emerge – some ultimate reality that is then belied by images. Philosophy, Deleuze argues, has usually taken this path, grounding all relations (AND, BECAUSE, OR) on being (IS). Classical cinema has also tended towards this path. Montage connects movements; we are no longer caught up in those movements (action and reaction) but we think the whole from which those movements emerge (as nature, or history, or national consciousness). Time, or the power for life to differ, is therefore read back from movement. This would be analogous to forms of contemporary poststructuralism where we acknowledge that we speak and think within some differentiated conceptual system, but that we can only know that system *as effected*, never as it is in itself.[50] A second transcendental path, rarely explored by philosophy, would be to think the externality of relations. If there is *no* being that determines relations, if each relation is produced on the basis of each new encounter, then *all* we have are connections and relations without prior ground: a series of 'ANDS' with no 'IS'. In cinema we approach this thought – this power to think the power of relationality, or firstness as such – only after thirdness:

> The mental image had not to be content with weaving a set of relations, but had to form a new substance. It had to become truly thought and thinking, even if it had to become 'difficult' in order to do this. *There were two conditions.* On the one hand, it would require and presuppose a putting into crisis of the action-image, the perception-image and the affection-image, even if this entailed the discovery of clichés everywhere. But, on the other hand, this crisis would be worthless by itself, it would only be the negative condition of the urpsurge of the new thinking image, even if it was necessary to look for it beyond movement.[51]

That is, we could remain within systems of relations, doing no more than charting operations of signs, with each perception of a system producing its own system and relation, and establishing yet one more point from which relations are viewed. This would give us Peirce's ever-expanding network of thirdness. Deleuze criticizes this aspect of Peirce's semiotics at the beginning of his second cinema book.[52] If Peirce had not simply accepted the three types of image 'as a fact' but had considered the emergence of those types – that is, how such orders or types are produced from firstness and how we can *think* both firstness and thirdness – he would have had to confront what Deleuze refers to as the 'interval'. Life is both the perception of forces among themselves, with each potential perception bearing some relation to the whole of life, *and* life is also the delay (or speed and slowness) of each perception responding to each other. While 'perception is strictly identical to every image, in so far as every image acts and reacts on all the others, on all their sides and in all their parts', we nevertheless have *action*. A body does not react immediately but pauses or vacillates between one possible reaction and another. Consider the difference between paint being thrown on a canvas and waves of light reaching the eye. The canvas receives the paint directly and changes immediately (becoming red or green); it neither acts upon, nor feels what it receives. The eye, by contrast, first feels *affect*; it alters in a way that does not just change what it is, but prompts it to move or respond – even if only to have a certain physiological response of boredom or disinterest. Affect *may* then issue in action, but what is crucial is the time between reception of light and movement: either the movement of affect or the time it takes to perceive the given, or the movement of action which is also temporally distanced from the perception of what one is reacting to. It is this delay or interval, a certain slowing down, which allows an agent or perceiver to emerge. The image I have of myself *as a self* is the effect of the fact that, unlike a molecular movement or perception, the relations I have with other movements around me are reflected: past images (memory) and relations (the image I have of the whole of life) will alter how I respond here and now. It is this *interval* which divides immediate action and reaction (what Deleuze refers to as a 'degree zero' of perception) from affects (where I feel but do not act) and acts (where I respond *for* this sense I have of what life ought to be):

> A special perception-image is therefore formed, an image which no longer simply expresses movement, but the reaction between movement and the interval of movement. If the movement-image is already perception, the perception-image will be perception of perception, and perception will have two poles, depending on whether it is identified with movement or with its interval (variation of all the images in their relations with each other, *or* variation of all the images in relation to one of them).[53]

The interval is of profound importance. The brain that delays the actions and reactions of the vast interconnected perceiving cosmos produces a zone of indetermination; what this body *will do*, the relations it *may* establish are not already given. Thus, the *essence* of a body is not its self-stabilizing nature but its power *not* to be what it already is, its potential to produce new (or non-intrinsic) relations. The interval is the virtual. The image to which I react is at once actual – my eye encounters the image and sees this here – but it is also virtual: I feel but do not act, or I recall another image that alters how I might respond. In addition to Peirce's three images of perception, affection and action, Deleuze therefore introduces another three which are poised in the interval. These are the impulse-image, which occurs *between* affection and action, the reflection-image, which is between action and relation, and then the relation-image as such, the image not of the interval between this or that, but an image of delay, pause or hesitation as such (the power of time). Deleuze insists that we can go beyond simply perceiving relations, beyond a cinema that sees a character seeing (dicisign) to what he refers to as the 'engramme'. This is not a *character* seeing; it is an impersonal seeing, freed from the human eye, freed from action, freed from a body that can chart movement from one point to another. This cinematic eye does not just depict the fluidity of movement (the 'reume'). In the engramme the camera has no fixed point or locus, so that moving images are combined with a moving camera. This comes close to giving us an image of time. Time is not the fixed point or now through which movements and moments are represented; once we are given different flows – such as the movement of the camera coupling with the movement of what is pictured – we are also given the multiple durations that time makes possible. Movements are only possible because time is the power or potential to change – not change of location (change within life) but change as alteration (the change that *is life*). In his non-cinematic works Deleuze constantly refers to singularities or potentialities that give relations, such that one is able to see the present not just as what is here and now, but also as what might be for other times, for other perceivers:

> The engramme, finally, is the genetic or the gaseous state of perception, molecular perception, which the two others presuppose. The affection-image has the *icon* as a sign of composition, which can be of a quality or power; it is a quality or power which is only expressed (for example, a face) without being actualized. But it is the *qualisign* or the *potisign* which constitute the genetic element because they construct quality or power in any-space-whatever, that is, in a space that does not yet appear as a real setting.[54]

Deleuze opens his second cinema book with this image that would present movement in genesis, and argues that the 'movement-image is matter itself'.[55] Matter, following Bergson, is one tendency of life, a tendency towards extension through time, or remaining the same.

Unlike mind or spirit, matter is deprived of the energy or life that would relate one point to another. If one takes one stone out of a box of stones the remaining stones stay the same, and stay as stones, and this is because each component of an actual multiplicity does not relate to any other component – everything is already given; a virtual or spiritual multiplicity, by contrast, changes in kind with every addition or division, and its processes of change are irreversible. My memory is *intensive* because each past event alters the present and each future event will alter how I relate to my past; matter is *extensive* because it does not synthesize or connect its differences. The bird flying across the sky, reflected in the flowing river, which also reflects the movements of clouds: if we were to picture these different durations or all the ways in which life flows at different speeds we would have a movement-image: not a matter that then moves, but matter as different styles of movement. However, the power to think these movements together is *spirit,* and it is only with the spiritual dimension that we can approach time directly.

CHAPTER 3

ART AND TIME

DESTRUCTION OF THE SENSORY-MOTOR APPARATUS AND THE SPIRITUAL AUTOMATON

If classical cinema went some way to freeing thought from its habits and clichés by presenting images of movements not reducible to a single located observer but referable to an open whole, modern cinema takes the alternate path of thinking the genesis of relations, not their subsumption in some overarching (albeit dynamic) nature or history. Time is no longer thought of as the totality of movements, even if that totality is never fully given (the 'open whole'). Time, far from being the series of movements (chronological time) becomes a *crack or fissure*: that which does not lead seamlessly from one point to another but disrupts wholeness, precludes an all-encompassing unity, and jolts the sensory-motor apparatus out of its closed circuit of human action.

To a great extent, then, Deleuze's 'history' of cinema is highly normative, and this because of his location of cinema within the history of thought and what thought *can do* but has so far failed to do. Thinking is not a coherent grasp and recognition of a set of facts. On the contrary, recognition is to a great degree a failure to think. We see this flux of movements or alterations not as a temporal becoming but as a set of things with stable qualities, and regard ourselves as subjects who might act upon these things (all the while remaining who we are). Thinking, for Deleuze however, is not coherence, continuity and recognition, but the interval: that we are *not* caused to do this or that, that we have no good nature that would determine in advance what sense we might make of the world. Instead of coming up with yet one more image of thought – 'man' as a rational animal, moral agent, self-causing subject or signifying being – cinema allows us to confront imaging as such, not the outcome of relations (the produced image of 'man') but relations in genesis, or what *might or might not become*. Modern cinema is therefore a cinema of the gap, the irrational cut – where one set of images is disrupted by another, with this next set bearing no internal, logical or habitual connection to the former.

Deleuze's privileging of non-narrative modern cinema is not reducible to a French avant-garde fancy for the shock of the new, the resistant and the difficult. It is grounded on a philosophical commitment to go beyond established systems of signs in order to intuit how signs are possible. Relations are effected from potentials to relate, from the power of the virtual. This is why, throughout his work, Deleuze insists on the infinitive, rather than the noun, as the grammar of essence: not what something *is* (its remaining the same) but a potential to connect ('to green . . .', 'to become'). Any actual set – this space of moving located bodies – is effected from powers; and these powers might also have created other sets, other spaces. Deleuze will therefore object to narrative cinema, for narrative tends to begin with characters who act or move *because of the way they are*, whereas for Deleuze there are possible actions, movements, feelings and affects from which character is created. A certain image of life, such as the desiring man of the early novel, operates as the origin of action and relations; we act this way because we are members of a humanity we all recognize and affirm. In *Moll Flanders* or *Robinson Crusoe* the desire for profit, acquisition and fortune motivates characters to act, and this also provides the motor for the narrative; the novel will end when fortune has been achieved.

This tendency to narrative continuity is not confined to premodernist art; contemporary moral philosophy often assumes that there is something like humanity, and then asks how we might act in order to fulfil our humanity. What happens in this metalepsis is that the effect – a produced image of 'man' as a being with a continuous nature – is substituted for the cause. For Deleuze, however, the *cause* of any image of man or humanity is *dis*continuity; the mind does not respond or react immediately to the world within which it moves, for it delays response and in so doing forms an image of itself. If, for example, the brain receives a stimulus but does *not* act, it produces *affect*, and this feeling or immobilization allows for the very slowing down of action which *is* the thinking self. Modern cinema takes the very event that made thought possible – the interval or delay – and gives it an image. There is a tendency for thinking *not* to think, and this is because our openness to the perceptions that further life must also be countered by a certain imperceptibility. We cannot be fully open to life; we must select and deflect from the world itself. The interval or gap is both what allows us to think – in the delay we form an image of the world, creating ourselves as souls in relation to that world – and also precludes us from thinking, for we ignore the differences and perceptions that would destabilize our ongoing point of view.

The gap between the actual – the effected, selected and specific perceived – and the virtual or perceivable that goes beyond a located time is confronted directly by what Deleuze refers to as the crystal-image. It is at this point in the history of cinema that thinking confronts its own power (the interval) and its *impotence*, for there is always a gap, fissure, crack, unthought, or *in*humanity which precludes us from being fully 'at one' with life. Life is, after all, only possible through *not* being itself – a life that remained, in itself, the same and fully given would no longer be *living*.

Modern cinema is therefore an extension of the possibility of classical cinema, which despite its connection of sets of movements in relation to an open whole nevertheless freed movement from a located practical observer. At the same time, modern cinema is also a disruption of the tendency towards narrative. Deleuze reads the various ways in which modern cinema opens thought to the power of the outside. If the actual perceived world – a space of relations relative to this observer living in this time – is the effect of an interval or delay, or a certain *not* seeing alongside a power of synthesis, then modern cinema's Outside is not another space within the world but the spacing or differential potential from which any world is assembled. This is confronted most directly in the crystal-image, where the actual and virtual are presented in the smallest possible circuit. All perception, unless it is the zero degree of an immediate relay, possesses a virtual dimension. I experience the actual world in terms of future potentials – how my body might move in this space, how others might see this space, how this space might be changed – and in terms of the past.

Memory is the clearest case of the imbrication of the virtual in the actual. The world encountered by my body, with all the sensible effects the world delivers, is 'doubled' by a virtual world: if I can swim through this water now it is because of all the waves I have encountered before. I experience this water now with the movements, orientation and ideas I have developed over my years of swimming.[1] My body is both composed of actual matter *and* these potential movements. Most memory takes this form of habit memory, where the past – which is virtual, for it remains real even when not recalled or presented – is vaguely intertwined with the present of newness. There are two distinct dimensions in habitual memory (the present perception and the past that orients the present) but these dimensions are experienced as a unity, indistinctly. But Deleuze, following Bergson, does not resign himself to this indistinction: yes, we may experience the present through habits (including conceptual or cultural schemas) but this does not mean that through enough effort or energy we might not separate the distinct powers of the virtual. Indeed, the only way in which there can be a genuine experience of the new is if we radically separate the singularity of the past. Let us go back to the swimming example. Imagine that I want to swim differently by learning butterfly instead of breaststroke. No amount of repetition of breaststroke will help me, so how do I open a new relation, break with habit and create a new relation to the water? I have to remember what it is to learn to swim, what it is to take on a habit. I have to feel the water as if for the first time, while the memory of what it is to learn to swim enables me to draw again on the power to learn, the power to create one's body as a swimming body. Instead of recollecting swimming in general – the habits bound up in my body and day-to-day life – I would have to relive, reactivate *and* transform the first encounter of the past. This form of memory is not the habit memory that allows the present to take on the form of the past; it is a singular memory that allows the past to break the lassitude of the present.

In his *Untimely Meditations* Nietzsche (1844–1900) drew a distinction between uses and abuses of history.[2] We abuse history when we repeat the past in order to remain the same, in order to avoid living. The archivist believes that the restoration and preservation of the past will save us from having to deal with the shock of the new. Indeed, identities that remain the same are produced by archives in which each addition merely *extends* what something already is; national archives maintain a sense of a nation, while literary archives add to our sense of the author. The more of the past we add to the archive the more secure we are in our knowledge of the past and the more we maintain continuity. For Nietzsche and Deleuze, however, the contrary is the case. We repeat the past in order to destroy the present, with what actually remains of the past – the images we have maintained – being torn apart by the virtual power of the past. Considered *according to its essence* an archive would not be the expansion of the present, or the present's picture of the past – say, adding ever more eighteenth-century poems to what we once took to be 'romanticism' in order that we might have a more accurate and sober reading of the past. On the contrary, the past is one expression of life's power to differ. The repetition of the past does not, and cannot, produce the same effects in each of its repetitions, and this is because of the reality of the virtual. A work of art, such as one of the great Romantic poems, has the potential to alter the direction of time. Whereas habit – reading one poem after another – allows each moment to take the same form as the other, singular memory takes a constitutive moment of the past and relives its constitutive power. The past is *one* way in which the virtual power of life expresses itself. If we repeat the past's *virtual* dimension we repeat its power to create time, not to fill time.

Consider the case of a great Romantic poem, such as William Wordsworth's *The Prelude* of 1805. One 'archival' response would be to demystify its greatness and singularity. If we read enough of the context we recognize that this work of genius and imaginative renewal actually expresses a historical context where many poems of this type were being written. Indeed, the poem's depiction of a spiritual and imaginative revolution is *actually* the displacement of concrete political conditions. The archivist returns the singular work to its context, sees it as the repetition and mutation of a broader historical movement, and in so doing brings the poem to relevance. So, we can now read *The Prelude* as a historical document, as part of a tradition of literature which continues to the present. By contrast, according to Nietzsche's idea of eternal return, which Deleuze develops throughout his work, every event is the expression of the power of life to differ. Certain events of art are monumental precisely because they do not repeat or consolidate their time but allow for a rethinking of time, a rethinking of the very nature of life. To repeat these works is to repeat the creative potentials from which they emerged. If something like Romanticism has become canonical, such that we no longer read Romantic poems as singular but immediately subordinate them to their context, then this should precisely urge us to repeat them with an even greater resistance. Why did *The Prelude* have the force that it did, such that it became definitive of a time? If we repeat *that* force of the text, its virtual force, then we tear it from its constituted time and open its constitutive time, its power to create time, not exist within time.

The past bears the potential to open itself again. The crystal-image in cinema offers a more impersonal, more open power of the virtual than the previous examples of memory or history. The singular memory that allows me to re-create my body and learn to swim anew, or the singular artwork that creates an image of its time, also have a tendency to habit; once we learn to swim anew this can become habit, and once an artwork creates a monument for its time we tend to repeat that form of time (instead of repeating its time-forming power). Not only is the crystal-image in cinema freed from a body, it is also not just the intrusion of 'a' memory or 'a' past but the disruption of the virtual as such.[3] Indeed, time is just this power for any image to be perceived both as it is here and now for me – the actual – *and* as a potential to create further relations for other perceivers, any perceiver whatever, in any time in any locale. If we see something as it is *and* as it will be, may have been and might still be, we grasp the image of time itself. This is achieved in cinema when we abandon theatre – a framed scene for a located observer – for the sake of *life*:

> One leaves the theatre to get to life, but one leaves it imperceptibly, on the thread of the stream, that is, of time. It is by leaving it that time gives itself a future. Hence the importance of the question: where does life begin? Time in the crystal is differentiated into two movements, but one of them takes charge of the future and freedom, provided that it leaves the crystal. Then the real will be created; at the same time as it escapes the eternal referral back of the actual and the virtual, the present and the past.[4]

Deleuze introduces Federico Fellini's cinema as exemplary of the crystal-image; each passage through Rome in *La Dolce Vita* (1960) is at once this scene here and now, and the recollection of a past of journeys, as well as the potential for futures not yet given.[5] But Deleuze sets his discussion of the time-crystal after two remarks that allow us to see both how cinema is important for a thought of life *and* how we need to bear in mind that it is the problem of life and not cinema as such which is Deleuze's main concern. First, Deleuze notes that the mirroring in the crystal-image is the power of art as such. Art presents a particular, an actuality, but at the same time that particular is a power or virtuality. Art is not the presentation of, say, a still life as the accurate representation of a fruit bowl in a particular time and place. Rather the presentation of an actuality – this fruit bowl – also creates or brings forth a singularity: what it is for this array of colours and forms to appear, what it is for an object to be framed and collected. This virtual power, or the capacity of art to allow the virtual to stand forth and stand apart from actuality, is more evident in modern non-representational art, where art as such is the affirmation of the false – not what the world *is*, but how reality's repetition always yields more than itself. The red on this canvas is at once material and actual – this paint here and now in its perishability – and virtual and singular, as a power 'to red', repeatable in infinite variations for all time. There have always, Deleuze notes, been references within art to the process of art – the play within the play, the painting of a painter painting a subject, the story told within a story, or the drama about an actor. In such cases art presents the power of presentation as such. It might seem that such instances give us the exhaustion or end of art, where art can no longer do anything but refer to itself. But Deleuze argues that the form of self-reference needs to be understood in terms of its potential, or its 'justification'. If there can be a play within a play or, in cinema, the image of an image – a character remembering, or an object reflected – this is because there can only be the original – the first play or the initial character – because life as such is the power to create, to dissimulate, to image, to be more than itself. The crystal-image gives us both the actual emergence and the power for that emerged form to be repeated or mirrored differently:

> . . . the work in the mirror and the work in the seed have always accompanied art without ever exhausting it, because art found in them a means of creation for certain special images. By the same token, the film within the film does not signal an end of history, and is no more self-sufficient than is the flashback or the dream: it is just a method of working, which must be justified from elsewhere. In fact, it is a mode of the crystal-image.[6]

Deleuze remarks, though, that these cinematic techniques – art within art, images of images, flashbacks – only expose what has always marked art: the power of the false, the power of releasing the virtual from the actual. If a character dies in a novel we read both about the death of this character and also of 'a' death, what it is to die, the singularity of death. Art brings the virtuality of life to presence. Life, for Deleuze, is not something that simply *is* – a fully given world whose qualities can then be read off and determined. Life is a power to become, a potential for multiple creations in any number of styles. For the most part, practical relations to the world reduce infinite becoming to a closed set of functions; we map an ordered world of relations from a stable but repeatable viewpoint. Art, however, repeats the events of this actualized world in order to release the further power that was not brought to actuality; this is the process of 'counter-actualization' or counter-effectuation. In a dance, for example, we are given not just this body moving here and now but an expression of what it is *to move*; the love story is not just this couple falling in love but an expression of the potential *to love*. Deleuze argues that all movement and relations, including love and dance, open out a world or set of relations; when that dance or rela- tion of love is included in a work of art, we are given an image of – we adopt a relation to – the power of relationality or virtuality as such. The aim of art is, Deleuze argues, to maintain the status of dance or mime – not this body performing this function in order to achieve this end, but this body creating itself as its own end; the depiction of art, mime, dance or play within art is therefore an image of life's power to create what is not given – an image of the virtual, of futurity, of time:

> Counter-actualization is nothing, it belongs to a buffoon when it operates alone and pretends to have the value of what could have happened. But, to be the mime of what effectively occurs, to double the actualization with a counter-actualization, the identification with a distance, like the true actor and dancer, is to give to the truth of the event the only chance of not being confused with its inevitable actualization. It is to give to the crack the chance of flying over its own incorporeal surface area, without stopping at the bursting within each body; it is, finally, to give us the chance to go farther than we would have believed possible. To the extent that the pure event is each time imprisoned forever in its actualiza- tion, counter-actualization liberates it, always for other times.[7]

TIME AND MONEY

After linking the crystal-image back to the striving of all art and all life, Deleuze moves forward to what appears at first to be a highly local remark regarding cinema and money. Before looking in detail at Deleuze's disquisition on the role of money in the cinema we need to bear in mind the more general relation between money and time. Money is a medium of exchange, allowing an exchange of substances – say, one object for another – to be liberated from a simple barter system. I can pay you now for what I need, and you can pay me later for what you need. Money allows the temporal deferral of exchange and does so by introducing a general equivalence, measuring things in terms of exchange value – no longer what they are in themselves or according to my needs, but what they might be worth for all others entering the system. In capitalism labour is exchanged for money, and to this extent human time becomes *measured by money*, so that money is a measure of time. But time also becomes completely subsumed by or reducible to money. Time is the substance of the labour market; we earn money in order to save time (by buying other workers' labour) and to spend time, for we need money for our leisure time: holidays, entertainment, drugs, restaurants, Hollywood movies are all commodities that allow our 'free time' to serve capitalist production. In *Anti-Oedipus* and *A Thousand Plateaus* Deleuze and Guattari distinguish capitalism by this feature of immanent subsumption. We no longer submit to an exploitative labour market because of some imposed belief – 'work harder and your reward will be in heaven' – but because there is *no* belief, nothing other than the axiom of capital – the desire to buy more, work more, earn more, have more. We no longer subject our lives *to* some value, becoming slaves of the despot, for our lives *are* the only value: so many hours of productive life, with desires for nothing other than the flows of capital. The problem of art and money lies in the relation between art's power for counter-actualization – the power to liberate life from fixed units – and art's submission to mediation – all the clichés or pre-given forms that reduce life to measured or mapped time. The problem of money brings into relief what art had always hinted at in the image of a *plot or conspiracy*. The idea of plot is that of a constituted order, a certain determination in advance of possible outcomes, a reduction of life to an already decided set of combinations:

> The cinema as art itself lives in a direct relation with a permanent plot [*complot*], an international conspiracy which conditions it from within, as the most intimate and most indispensable enemy. The conspiracy is that of money; what defines industrial art is

not mechanical reproduction but the internalized relation with money.[8]

For Deleuze, films about money, such as Wim Wenders's *The State of Things* (1982), which presents a film crew fragmented and dispersed by a monetary 'plot whose key is elsewhere', are films about film (and therefore films about the relation between art and life). Films are, at their limit, confrontations with time. We can have an immobilized world only if we regard the images we perceive now as *the same* as the images we have perceived and will perceive. The stability of the world depends upon a seamless, equivalent and commensurable flow of images – a spatialized or chronological time, where the present 'now' is a variant of the past 'now', and where the future will be a development and variation of this present. If cinema disrupts that localization of images by presenting disjunct and fractured cuts we lose equalized, homogenized, spatialized and metric time. We lose the time of money: the time where the future is the same as the past, differing only in degree but submitted to one common measure. Capital pays me for what I do, giving me an amount for my time, which ensures that tomorrow will be equivalent to today. Capital thrives on the wager of time.

Money has always been the measuring, equalizing and ordering of time, and the very structure of human experience has always tended towards some form of unifying measure through time (which is why Deleuze and Guattari will argue in *Anti-Oedipus* that there has always been a tendency towards capitalism in all social relations). If I spend more time working *now* than I need to in order to live – if I invest time either in harvesting more food, or even thinking of more complex concepts – then I create the possibility for a different and less laborious future. What happens with *capitalism* is that the excess work I do now does *not* mean that I work less later on; rather, my surplus is used to create more work, for the capitalist will reinvest profits into more factories, more production. There is no site for waste, excess or anti-production. Pre-capitalist cultures might have had some point of anti-production, such as the squandering displays of royal festivals, but in capitalism all excess is reinvested. Money, or the conversion of all excess labour into a single measure, allows for one system of continual reinvestment – one axiom – that has no outside. Today, for example, we could look at any form of seeming waste and excess – such as corporate investments in communities, art projects or charities – but also be aware that such expenditure can ultimately be calculated. The corporation improves its image, creating cultural capital and increasing the intensity of production and consumption; excess is now one more commodity. At its simplest, if I create and produce more than I need in order to live – if I produce to excess – then I *might* alter the intensity of my life. Art is excess, not just what I need to survive but what might render me different.

All art has its material limits but cinema is the art of an industrial age and is tied crucially to the capitalist system of exchange. When a film confronts the plot of money it becomes a film about film, a film about the way in which time is subjected to measure. In this sense Deleuze differs from modernist artists who lamented the commodification of art simply because art would become popular; the problem with art's relation to money is, for Deleuze, more formal. Any art which aims to *reproduce* the future on the basis of the past is *majoritarian* and focuses on content: so we make sure that we have the next *Harry Potter*, the next *Star Wars* and the next *Big Brother* – repeating what has been expressed. Instead we should be striving to repeat the form, asking what book will change the landscape of children's literature, what film will create a new style of science fiction, what form of media will alter our way of thinking and living in the way that reality television has done. For Deleuze, then, cinema or art is great not when it maintains or repeats what has already been expressed, allowing content to circulate while leaving the system unchanged; great art changes the very nature of the system. Could a film about cinema and money make us think differently about our consumption of cinema, make us *see* differently? Deleuze is not opposed to popular film because it becomes common and then makes money; he is opposed to the idea that 'high' art strives to be elitist or explicitly resists market values.[9] On the contrary, he creates a new way of thinking the opposition between high/elitist art and popular/commercial art. Great art disrupts the pre-given categories through which we think; it is minor, not because it is enjoyed by an elite, but because it does not yet have a people or group whose world it represents. On such a reading there could be major elite authors – say, the consecrated works of a poet laureate – and major popular authors – such as the novels of Stephen King imitators or *Da Vinci Code* aspirants. But there could also be minor elite authors, such as Deleuze's cited example of Kafka, who needs to be read as one who did *not* belong to an identifiable literary community, *and* minor popular authors: we might cite here some of the great feminist-consciousness-raising books of the 1970s such as Germaine Greer's *The Female Eunuch* that created the group of women to whom it was addressed.[10]

For Deleuze it is *not* the case that machinic repetition and subjection to the market robs the work of its individuality and aura. Deleuze's insistence on singularity emphasizes that something *is* only insofar as it can differ and be repeated with variation. A great novel is a work that can be perverted, dramatized, disseminated into other cultures, misread by later epochs, transformed into modern cinematic versions; and the novel will be all the greater insofar as it allows for deviation. The problem of *money* in relation to art is not that works become separated from their aura, capable of being copied, distributed and torn from their origin. The problem lies in the style of repetition. Capitalism does have a tendency for deterritorialization, allowing any work to circulate, depart from its original productive intent and be varied infinitely, flowing across cultures, classes and sites of ownership. The very mechanism that allows for profit and commodification – that a work can be repeated efficiently and indefinitely, allowing the original producer to maximize the energy of his original work – is the same mechanism that allows for circulation without profit or return. In the case of music copying, for example, the recording technology that allows a work to be repeated as the same, copyrighted and circulated in a network of exchange (territorialization, or the creation of an assemblage of market relations) also allows for the dispersal of energy and aberrant repetition; bootlegs, illegal downloads, piracy and corruption are extensions of the very processes that allow art to become profitable in the first place. The role of *money* in circulation and repetition is one of *re*territorialization; all copying, circulation and dissemination occur not for the sake of creating a difference or new relations, but for reinforcing the circulation of money. One creates a sequel to *Bridget Jones's Diary* in order to repeat the same networks of exchange, in order to have the original flows of money, audience and products repeated in the same way. The point for Deleuze is not to resist the repetition and circulation of art, but to allow that circulation to proceed without the reterritorialization of money: the creation of a sequel that would repeat the creative force of the original, not its effected relations of exchange. In *What is Philosophy?* Deleuze and Guattari argue that philosophy is not a reaction against capitalism, nor some attempt to establish a point of truth beyond the circulation of difference or anti-foundationalism of capitalism, but an extension of capitalism's tendency *beyond money*:

> Philosophy takes the relative deterritorialization of capital to the absolute; it makes it pass over the plane of immanence as movement of the infinite and suppresses it as internal limit, *turns it back against itself so as to summon forth a new earth, a new people.*[11]

When cinema comes up against the logic of money, when in the most brutal manner the making of a film grinds to a halt because money has run out, we are not, Deleuze insists, looking at an external intrusion. On the contrary, we are again brought face to face with life's struggle with *time*. Money is both possible because of time *and* a reduction of the radical potential of time. As modern cinema shows, movements are not alterations of things within space, but powers to become, create and connect *from which spaces and relatively immobile 'blocks of becoming'* are formed. Money is possible because of this always altering temporality; we do not exchange one thing for another immediately but allow all things to be subject to *possible* exchange in terms of a unit that remains the same through time. The system of money reduces the openness of relations and production to exchange. Art is a bet with time: who knows what powers might be released by this event if it is repeated beyond the actual system, if the work is released without strict regard for monetary return? Money is the taming of time, returning the experimentation with images to the order of the present. Money is at once a *de*territorialization which allows relations to extend beyond immediate exchange or barter, thereby extending a tendency of life to create or produce for what is not present; but it is also a reterritorialization which introduces equivalence, sameness and a quantity of value through time, an attempt to contain and master the disequilibrium of time.

While cinema bears a potential to liberate time from a reduction to equivalence, and achieves this emancipation of time by opening relations not already determined by any single image, money closes off that opening, preventing cinema from being an absolutely open and undetermined production of relations:

> This is the old curse which undermines the cinema: time is money. If it is true that movement maintains a set of exchanges or an

equivalence, a symmetry as an invariant, time is by nature the conspiracy of unequal exchange or the impossibility of an equivalence. It is in this sense that time is money: in Marx's two formulations, C-M-C is that of equivalence, but M-C-M is that of impossible equivalence or tricked dissymmetrical exchange.[12]

In the first formula – C-M-C – money mediates or renders equivalent the relations of capital; in the second – M-C-M – the flows of money move through capital, so that what appears equivalent (money) is different according to what is being circulated (flows of objects). Deleuze sees the confrontation with money, or the taming of time that would reduce all movements to one system of relations, as the moment in cinema when time appears for itself. In the film within the film, where the film does not get made because of the lack of money, we directly confront the halting of image production through the fixation on one moving image, the movement of money. Cinema is only possible because there is a potential for life to produce points of view or technologies not grounded in actual life: the invention of the camera, which opens a world different from the human body. But cinema is also only possible when this deterritorialization is coupled with a system of money and profit which powers its development; these two tendencies for virtual creation on the one hand and codification of that creation in the unit of money on the other, are directly represented in those films that confront time and money:

> In short, the cinema confronts *its most internal presupposition, money, and the movement-image makes way for the time-image in one and the same operation* . . . The film is movement but the film within the film is money, is time.[13]

By presenting the image of the very production of a set of images cinema gives a direct confrontation with time. Time is no longer that which measures movement within the world, but is the creation of images that alter just what counts as the world. Cinema presents an image of the opening of relations of another world from within an actual world. This is time: the production of worlds, not the passage from one moment to another 'in' time, but the opening of time, the creation of the new. Money as inflation is time, the incapacity of the present system of exchange to maintain sameness and equilibrium precisely when there is anticipation or speculation regarding a future not yet given:

> What the film within expresses is this infernal circuit between the image and money, this inflation which time puts into the exchange, this 'overwhelming rise' . . . The crystal-image thus receives the principle which is its foundation: endlessly relaunching exchange which is dissymmetrical, unequal and without equivalence, giving image for money, giving time for images, converting time, the transparent side, and money, the opaque side, like a spinning top on its end. And the film will be finished when there is no more money left . . . [14]

Money is only possible because of the virtual – anticipation, speculation and the doubling of the object with its value – but money also *reduces* the virtual by coding relations and the future in terms of one system or circuit; the crystal-image, which presents an image of the object and its potential at one and the same time, is therefore the disclosure of the principle of money, and the liberation of that principle from closed exchange.

Time is the impossibility of a single closed economy, the impossibility of grasping, from various movements, an image of a whole or fixed plane. There is no plane within which, or from which, movement takes place; time is the unfolding of movement, not the measure or container of movement. Time, is therefore, multiple. This is because time is not some overarching unity *in which* all things find their place; time is dis-unity, non-equivalence, chaos and fracture – the multiplicity of durations. The time-image in cinema is the confrontation with that which does not remain itself from one moment to another; everything is at once itself (actual) and a potential for difference not reducible to the now:

> Time consists of this split, and it is this, it is time, that *we see in the crystal*. The crystal image was not time but we see time in the crystal. We see in the crystal the perpetual foundation of time, non-chronological time, chronos and not Chronos. This is the powerful, non-organic Life which grips the world. [15]

CHAPTER 4

ART AND HISTORY

MONUMENT

Philosophy's concepts, Deleuze insists, are not abstractions: we do not look at all the instances of justice and then define justice as a generality. Rather, a philosophical concept allows us to think of the power or potential that would make an act of actual justice possible. This is why the concept moves at *infinite speed*. It does not look here at one case, there at another, and come up with an average or set of cases that might then be added to. The concept grasps *at once* intertwined relations. Justice is a certain connection or power of moving between action, effect, social body, judgment, will, impartiality and order. When we ask of an act whether it is just we do not have a separate external standard to which we compare it, but we do have a way of thinking the act: what does it do, what is its style? Justice would be the balance of forces actualized in an act. Deleuze, for example, considers the concept of the *cogito*, established by Descartes on the basis that if I am thinking, then the one thing I cannot doubt is that I am thinking; therefore the *ego cogito* or 'I think' establishes the immediate relation between thinking and being a certain, subsistent and self-present subject.[1] These features are not added on to the concept of a thing, for they *are* the concept in their immediate relation to each other. The *cogito* may be defined in a series of steps, but Descartes creates a concept in which thinking, doubting, being certain of oneself and being a self are all immediately connected. Similarly, we might say that while philosophy has defined the concept of justice in different ways, the problem of justice immediately links judging, acting, rightness, order and sociality; any definition begins from this plane or orientation of the problem. In working with a concept philosophy may make so many new connections as to inaugurate an entirely new plane. There can be disputes about the nature of reason within a plane – is reason innate or acquired? – but there can also be new concepts of reason that demand a whole new plane: this might occur if we thought of reason in terms of inhuman calculations of computers or other artificial intelligence machines. There have been disputes about justice, such as the first book of Plato's *Republic*, which debate whether justice is a norm that transcends human judgment; but there have also been critical interventions which define the concept of justice so radically that it creates a new inhuman plane of philosophy. When Derrida suggests that justice is not reducible to any human action, nor can be given any present form, he creates a concept that is explicitly not extensive – a generalization of all those things we take to be just. Rather, it is intensive in Deleuze's sense, for it opens a potential movement: how would we think and act if we could imagine a justice that was pure, infinite and uncorrupted?[2] The concept is, therefore, the power of thinking to *survey* the movement of life, not being located within the lived but grasping a certain aspect of the lived *all at once*: what is thinking as such, justice as such, reason as such? Before we have objects that we perceive to be the same through time and to be similar in nature – the generalizations of the intellect that allow for efficient action – we have to have some milieu of sense. It is this milieu or power of thinking the present in terms of what it offers 'for all time' that enables the creation of concepts.

In a similar but distinct way to his theory of concepts as intensive and surveying, Deleuze also insists on art as a power that is not located within lived experience, nor within a constituted, personal or historical time. Whereas the ultimate ground of a phenomenology of concepts and art is experience – or a time that constitutes itself by synthesizing a before with an after in a flowing present – Deleuze and Guattari unground art through their notions of percept and affect. Percepts and affects are *not* continuous with life and are not effects of a synthetic activity of consciousness. Affects and percepts stand alone and bear an autonomy that undoes any supposed independence of self-constituting consciousness: 'we attain to the percept and the affect only as to autonomous and sufficient beings that no longer owe anything to those who experience them or who have experienced them'.[3] No art, then, is representational – bearing a resemblance to the world: 'no art and no sensation have ever been representational'.[4] Nor is art expressive of an author's personal vision. If art is expressive it is expressive of matter: 'matter becomes expressive'.[5] And when matter becomes expressive it opens out away from its actualized extension to release its eternal potential: not matter as it is organized through our located experience, but matter in its power to be experienced differently, beyond our point of view. Art is monumental in the sense of standing alone, producing sensations that no longer rely on a perceiving subject or a constituted world. On the one hand, Deleuze and Guattari create a unique reading of modernist aesthetics to make this point. For they at once draw upon modernism's insistence that art is not reducible to everyday life or human experience, but they take this separation of art beyond modernism's location of the art object within some broader concept of humanity or tradition. Whereas modernism often separated art from everyday enjoyment and communication, modernists often appealed to history, tradition or culture as the broader life that might be appealed to in the face of commodification. Deleuze and Guattari reject the idea that there is some human history or tradition which might reground life and which can be retrieved if art is separated from everyday life. Great art is minor precisely because it is not expressive of any already constituted tradition, and the life which the work opens is radically inhuman and radically futural – not yet given any form or experience.[6] On the other hand, while critical of some aspects of modernism, it is the modernist production of the radically separate artwork that enables Deleuze and Guattari to see the autonomy of affect and percept in *all* art (just as the advent of cinema allows us to think of the virtuality in all images, and the advent of capitalism proper allows us to recognize the flows of production in all life).

There is one way in which we could think the relation between modernism and the philosophies of meaning upon which Deleuze draws. Both Bergson and Husserl were critical of a modern systematized life that had reduced experience to mechanistic, efficient and repetitive movement and had forgotten the animating life from which systems and maps of movement emerge. Modernist art could, similarly, be read as a radically historicizing gesture critical of clock-time, habit, reification, commodification and the reduction of tradition to so much manipulable data and circulating dead objects. The great modernist works of literature stepped back from the ordered present in order to intuit the emergence of order from chaos, the genesis and sense of logic from the flux of life. It is this image of plunging back into life and then re-emerging with the work of art that frames Ezra Pound's *Cantos*, which recalls Homer's *Odyssey* and the poet's giving of blood to the ghosts of the past in order to retrieve the life of the present.[7] Everyday present life is dead precisely because it has become enslaved to the technologies that were originally formed to sustain life. In T. S. Eliot's *The Waste Land* urban commuters are figured as the march of the dead into hell: 'I had not thought death had undone so many.' In D. H. Lawrence's novels and short stories, mining communities are represented as a form of living dead. In Joyce's *Ulysses* a funereal body passes through the streets of London, and in Virginia Woolf's *Mrs Dalloway* the city is haunted by the spectral figure of Septimus, the returned soldier. For the modernists, the only way out of this land of the living dead is through an escape from life as it is currently lived. Deleuze and Guattari directly refer to this communion with the dead in *What is Philosophy?* In place of the life that has become ordered by the labouring, organized and efficient human body Deleuze and Guattari celebrate a life of sensations that are not yet synthesized or rendered meaningful, not yet reduced to finite and manageable units:

> The philosopher, the scientist, and the artist seem to return from the land of the dead. . . . The artist brings back from the chaos *varieties* that no longer constitute a reproduction of the sensory in the organ but set up a being of the sensory, a being of sensation, on an organic plane of composition that is able to restore the infinite.[8]

Just as Joyce's *Ulysses* sets the flowing life of Molly Bloom's menstruation beyond the newspaper-dominated streets of urban Dublin, and Eliot sets the passage of the Thames beyond the disembodied voices of the gramophone and radio, so Woolf also describes the imaginative stroll of Clarissa Dalloway as constantly broken by the intrusion of the tolling of clock-time. Deleuze and Guattari, embracing this modernist appeal to a life and time beyond mechanized experience, also describe the artist as plunging into chaos and returning with a renovated order:

> Through having reached the percept as 'the sacred source,' through having seen life in the living or the living in the lived, the novelist or painter becomes breathless and with bloodshot eyes.[9]

Deleuze's approach to modernism is not, however, reducible to a return to the 'lived', and this is where Deleuze differs most not only from Bergson and phenomenology but also from the mythic strands of modernism that regard the return of the artist from chaos as the reconstitution of meaning, unity and humanization. Whereas Husserl considered mathematics and logic to be the sciences which best brought experience back to its potential to intuit the truth of life, the phenomenological tradition that followed him privileged art. Heidegger argued that in the work of art we are brought to the 'worlding' of the world, no longer seeing objects before us as simply present or 'there' but becoming aware of how the world is brought to presence or disclosed.[10] The categories and habits we accept as already given should be seen to be *acts* of consciousness or events of existence from which the distinction between subject and object is then effected. Even Bergson's insistence on thinking the durations from which the human body creates a single centre nevertheless privileged the *human* capacity to transcend interested viewpoints and imagine humanity in general, a humanity for all time. Not only did T. S. Eliot regard modernism as a restoration of a world that had fallen into a panorama of futility, Joyce also located all the disparate and equivocal voices of tradition within one flowing, bodily life. Deleuze, by contrast, insists that art releases what *stands alone*, and here he refers to Virginia Woolf, the least panoramic, epic or totalizing of all literary modernists.

Referring to Woolf, Deleuze and Guattari raise the problem of the moment: 'How can a moment of the world be rendered durable or made to exist for itself?'[11] As in his cinema books Deleuze gives detailed, formal, concrete and specific accounts of how artistic material can release autonomous percepts and affects. But the *possibility* of such artistic techniques and endeavours lies in Deleuze's ontology of life. Life is not 'the lived', not the unified world of one ongoing, meaning-producing humanity. On the contrary, there can only be the perception of the life of humanity or the history of this world because various affects have been organized from some synthesizing point of view; before the 'lived' there is, for Deleuze and Guattari, the affects or possible encounters from which lives are forged: 'The affect certainly does not undertake a return to origins, as if beneath civilization we would rediscover, in terms of resemblance, the persistence of a bestial or primitive humanity.'[12] Life is a multiplicity of powers to differ,[13] so that matter is expressive *not only* in its encounter with the human eye (the actually perceived, or perceptions) but also in its autonomous, vibrating and inhuman power (the virtual percept, what is there *to be perceived*).

This is why for Deleuze and Guattari all art is monument and stands alone; the red on a canvas is selected from the lived world (where red is the colour of some being with a particular location and function), but the *selection* takes colour from its practical context, allowing it to be perceived as such. Further, Deleuze looks at the way art selects matter, removes it from its everyday context of action and meaning, and then brings matter into contact with that other tendency of life – spirit. For the most part, we experience life in a combination of these two tendencies; my material body is organized through my intentions and perceptions, so that all matter is lived not as it is in its power to stand alone, but as it is *for me*. In art, however, this composition is broken down and we live matter as that which can come to be spiritualized. There are two tendencies of life. The first is matter, which tends towards space and extension (or existing non-relationally, separate and without reference to its potentials or what it might become). The second is spirit, which connects with what is not already actual and allows for the relation to possibility, or what might become. In art we can see matter as it is in itself coming into contact with powers of expression, or powers to unfold differences that are not given. In William Blake's engravings, for example, Blake combines the rigid materiality of lines – manifestly cut into a resisting material – with the figure of bodies in movement, showing the ways in which the body's desire or dynamism brings matter into movement or expression.[14] William Blake provides a clear example of the problem of art as it is outlined in Deleuze's work on Francis Bacon. Blake combined an engraving of lines in copper plates – a form of expression – with depicted bodies in movement – a form of content.[15] His work therefore displayed the ways in which the material with which he worked, such as the copper plate, the wax drawn on that plate, the acid used to corrode the unwaxed plate, and then the colour painted on to that paint, already took on a form of its own; but this form of expression then had to encounter the form of content, which for Blake consisted of bodies with emphasized musculature, dynamic movement and exaggerated facial expression. What we see in Blake is *not* a message that could have been conveyed in some other medium, but the matter of the medium itself that 'stands alone' and creates a singular encounter when it struggles to release an image of the human form, as though Blake captured *in the material* the affect of the body's own struggle with movement. I choose this example because Blake's images are readily available on the Internet, even though the reproduced images miss the differences that Blake achieved with each repeated printed plate, and miss the textural quality that followed from Blake's heavy use of colour on some plates.[16]

Matter is expressive in all art, including an art of colourism that would try to present, say, red as it is in itself in its power to be perceived or to produce perceptions, and including abstractionism, where forms are detached from actual bodies and we are given powers of line or relation; but Deleuze's direct preference is for neither colourism nor abstraction but expressivism, where we see the difference of two tendencies that are indistinct in everyday life, the tendency towards spirit or creating what is not given, and the tendency of matter which is to conserve and retain the merely given. It is only because art is not bound up with life as it is actualized – not coordinated with our actions in the way of traffic signals, trained responses and habits – that it has the power to open the virtual.

By separating the tendencies of matter from the tendencies of spirit, art releases us from life as it is lived efficiently and productively, and opens life to what it might become. Here, as elsewhere, Deleuze's thought confronts what he continually refers to as the externality of relations. Life is not properly realized in human perception, for our 'world' is only *one* of the ways in which life might be actualized or lived. The power of the artist is to take an actualized set of relations – the lived – and open the potential of other relations. Here one does not grasp life in itself, nor the humanity from which any meaningful life is constituted. Rather, art presents life as a power to vary, as the potential for colour, light or line to produce sensations other than those already lived: 'The artist is always adding new varieties to the world. Beings of sensation are varieties, just as the concept's beings are variations, and the functions of being are variables.'[17] Once sensation is liberated from a produced relation, or sensation as it is lived, we reach sensation as it stands alone, the vibration or *power to differ* of life from which relations are effected: 'sensation in itself'.[18] It is not, then, that art reactivates consciousness, recalling the disclosure and synthesis of the world by the subject. Deleuze and Guattari set themselves against the idea that the work of art brings us back to some original condition of world-disclosure or meaning-making with which we have lost touch; art is not nostalgia or self-recollection. For art is one of the ways in which thought approaches infinite speed. If we have a subject–object relation because the body does not act immediately but pauses or slows down to decide how to act, and does so by fixing an image of the world that remains the same through time, then art can approach sensation itself only by releasing the perceptual apparatus from acting on the world. We no longer have this extended world as it is for me and my possible actions. One does not establish a point of practical interest that would 'frame' the world in terms of the needs of this human body. For in *not* acting, or in contemplating life passively – not being a self or 'becoming-imperceptible' – life is no longer folded around a specific point of view but is disclosed in its power to create varied relations: 'Contemplating is creating, the mystery of passive creation.'[19]

Deleuze's connection of art with life differs subtly from a certain interpretation of modernism and from a more general privileging of the *act* in Western thought. One of the horrors and nightmare visions of modernism was the loss of humanization and active reason in the face of an increasingly inhuman, chaotic, meaningless and fragmented world; the artist would therefore be supreme artificer, once more creating a world whose genesis from human meaning and relations had been forgotten. In this regard, modernism would be complicit with a Western tradition that turns away from the contingent inhumanity of the world and elevates the image of life as meaningful, end-oriented and self-expressive action. If God is defined as that perfect being who is pure act, not determined by anything other than his own essence, humans become more like God the more they bring themselves into being. The work of art, on this understanding, would be both the expression and the result of human self-constitution. Human beings create themselves and actualize their full potential through the act of creation; the art-object is the expression of 'human-becoming'. By contrast, Deleuze's definition of art as *monument* puts forward a radically impassive image of life. Against the idea of a God that has no being (no essence) other than the pure act of self-actualization, Deleuze's entire philosophy of the virtual affirms what does not act, is not actualized or brought to presence, and has yet to realize itself through effected relations. Contemplation, sensation in itself, pure affects and percepts – all these are names for those powers of life that are *not* synthesized into active and productive unities. Deleuze is opposed to the existential emphasis on human life that 'is' only in its *not* being itself, in its capacity to create itself *ex nihilo*. In this sense Deleuze is also directly opposed to vitalism or the reference of all that is possible back to some grounding self-constituting life; what is important is not the unfolding *of life* (where life would be some ultimate pseudo-theological agent or subject), so much as the power of life to create folds that are not its own, unforeseen and ungrounded:

> Vitalism has always had two possible interpretations: that of an idea that acts, but is not – that acts therefore only from the point of view of an external cerebral knowledge . . . or that of a force that is but does not act – that is therefore a pure internal aware-ness . . . If the second interpretation seems to us to be imperative it is because the contraction that preserves is always in a state of detachment in relation to action or even to movement and appears as a pure contemplation without knowledge.[20]

Deleuze and Guattari draw here upon Bergson's *Creative Evolution*. Mind and matter are two trajectories that emerge from the tendency of life. In order to move forward, life must expend energy in an explo-sive and differing force. On the other hand, in order to move forward effectively, life also delays expenditure and contemplates how it will act, allowing for the formation of habits and regularities that save energy and ultimately time. Life is therefore both expenditure (acting immediately, not thinking) and reserve (not acting, pausing, thinking, contemplating in order that one might move efficiently with less time). We can also think of this in terms of the relaxation or extension or matter, where all is given at once – we experience the stone as matter if it is one of many stones and we know fully what it can do and be – in opposition to the contraction of spirit, which is perceived as not fully given or reserved, for we experience other minds as different from each other in their capacity to act differently in ways not already given. If, however, contemplation of spirit slows completely and does *not act at all* then the contraction of spirit allows for an image of sensation itself: not sensation in order to act, but sensation that is as an encounter with the souls or powers that are not our own. The eye becomes not an organ within a body that orders sensation according to its needs and motility, but nothing other than the sensation it enjoys:

> Contraction is not an action but a pure passion, a contemplation that preserves the before in the after. Sensation, then, is on a plane

that is different from mechanisms, dynamisms and finalities: it is a plane of composition where sensation is formed by contracting that which composes it, and by composing itself with other sensations that contract it in turn. Sensation is pure contemplation, for it is through contemplation that one contracts, contemplating itself with other sensations that contract it in turn.[21]

FRAMING, TERRITORIALIZATION AND THE PLANE OF COMPOSITION

How, then, is such contemplation achieved? How do we achieve that event whereby the image is not grasped as the image *of* some thing for some observer, so there is just seeing, sensation? Deleuze here draws on architectural and cinematic movements, both of which allow us to imagine a seemingly static work of art within time (such as a book or canvas) as an opening out on to a time of becoming – from chronological time, where one moment follows another, to the time of Aion, or a 'for all time'. One sees the sensation *as such* in its potential to be repeated, varied and actualized in a multiplicity of times. The frames of cinema select a scene of movement. This enables a movement-image whereby the motion produces space: space is given as that which is crossed or traversed by movement. There is not a space in which things move, but movements that compose a non-homogeneous space. In the time-image, framed movement halts the interested sequence of history and action and presents movement as a power to produce a multiplicity of relations in a multiplicity of times; the close-up, for example, gives us the face *as affected*, and so it remains open as to what will happen, what will be felt, articulated or done. This contemplative power of art does not, of course, reside in cinema alone. All art is an isolation of an affect or percept – separated from the ordered world – that then allows for the opening of an infinite: art wants to create the finite that restores the infinite; it lays out a plane of composition that, in turn, through the action of aesthetic figures, bears monuments or composite sensations.[22] A canvas is the framing, not of a scene to be represented, but a selection of the plane of composition. What is seen is not the world as it is coloured, as though sensibilities were qualities through which we grasped being. Rather, colours, textures, shadows, lines and figures *are* the being of the world. It is not, as Deleuze points out in *Difference and Repetition*, that being has a sensible dimension ('the sensibility of being'); for being *is* the sensible ('the being of the sensible'). Colours, lights, sounds, planes, lines and textures are presented as the powers or potentials that allow us to perceive worlds. So colour, in the work of art, has to be extracted from the plane of composition – presented not as a perceptual overlay, but as one connection through which being is given. We only have colours because of the forces of light and sensation that encounter each other, just as we only have geometrical form through the encounter of space with sections, and we only have the texture of a canvas through the encounters of light with depth and thickness:

> By means of the material, the aim of art is to wrest the percept from perceptions of objects and the states of a perceiving subject, to wrest the affect from affections as the transition from one state to another: to extract a bloc of sensations, a pure being of sensations.[23]

In all cases, art's achievement is to present the world we perceive and feel as the result of that which is *there to be perceived*, and *to be felt*. Somehow – and this will vary from artist to artist – the material, the paint on the canvas, has to capture within time and space, the intensities, singularities or powers which open spaces and which are then perceived in chronological time. Such singularities are, in this sense, 'for all time' or 'untimely'; they bear a power to be actualized over and over again, returning eternally.

The plane of composition opened by an artwork cannot be identified as an origin, ground or founding subject. This is a crucial feature of all Deleuze and Guattari's work, which ties them both to a modernist conception of art *and* distinguishes them from either a philosophy of life or phenomenology. We can understand this by looking at the 'plane of composition' more concretely in terms of a modernist aesthetic, and then looking at how Deleuze's aesthetic modernism radicalizes philosophy.

Consider a standard definition of postmodern art as ironic,[24] dehistoricized,[25] parodic,[26] flat, metafictional,[27] quotational and multivocal.[28] Postmodern literary works adopt received voices, repeating clichés, slogans, quotations and myths. Postmodern visual works paste together advertising images, iconic images from history, street signs, soup labels, bodily products and mass-produced kitsch. If there is an *idea* of postmodern art it is that there is nothing outside the circulation of images; our only critical position is to repeat already constituted signs *as signs*. Texts that are about writing, that refer to their own process of production – such as those of Italo Calvino – demystify the notion of an author outside the work; the author becomes one voice among others in a completely flat pastiche, where signs are no longer signs *of* some world. While both modernist and postmodernist works are often dominated by fragments or sections, having eschewed narrative continuity and authorial centres, Deleuze focuses on the specific nature of the artwork's capacity to allow matter to stand alone. The art works favoured by Deleuze are, therefore, frequently modernist, and – while as reflexive as the most distanced postmodern works – go well beyond quotation and aim to confront the 'being of the sensible'. In his book on Francis Bacon, for example, Deleuze looks closely at the ways in which the canvases work with the relation between figure and ground, with Deleuze insisting that this negotiation of materials is a style of thinking, a way of working through the potentials of matter and powers of differentiation (just as a philosopher creates concepts to differentiate movements or essences). The plane of composition, in the visual arts, comprises powers that open a field of vision, but do so in a way that we have a sense of the visual opening as such. Thus, a colourist varies a colour, exposing all the potentialities of red, such that the colour we see now in all its variants is a power to be seen (and varied) again and anew for all time. A canvas that selects a frame of colour, such as a Cy Twombly canvas that is white paint textured and layered, gives us the power of white; we can say that the essence is given *not* in presenting this colour as it is, but presenting its power and potential for variation – to be seen here and now, and as it might be for other times in other variations. By varying colour, or line, or form or figure, we see each visual predicate not as the quality that is attached to a substance – x is white – but as a power through which being is expressed: 'being' is composed of powers *to differ*, what Deleuze early on referred to in *The Logic of Sense* as 'pure predicates'. In his book on Francis Bacon, Deleuze affirms both Bacon and Cezanne's release of the 'spatializing energy of colour'.[29] In so doing he rejected the idea of qualities *through which* we grasp some underlying being, and instead insisted that 'being' is nothing other than a power to express itself in variation or difference, with each difference being less the expression *of* some preceding or grounding substance and more the capacity to respond to multiple connections.

For this reason Deleuze, in *Difference and Repetition*, wrote of '?being'. In a work of visual art we encounter the powers of expression through percepts and affects – powers of being perceived (such as this white in its capacity to be seen both now and as it will be for other times, in unfolding variation) and powers of being affected (the shocks, vibrations and sensations that may unfold into action). In a canvas, such as Twombly's, a territory is created that frames variations – white in its power to differ. But if art achieves its potential this is because we think through the percept. Art does not represent in paint what we might otherwise represent in concepts; art thinks in its own way. In the case of a canvas of colour, thinking colour itself, in its perceivability, releases us from the idea of a world of neutral substance that is *then* overlaid by qualities: not a world that is 'in itself' and which is then related to a viewer through perceptions. Rather, the isolation of percepts allows us to live a world that *is* relation and variation, where predicates or qualities are the outcome of encounters. There is not a space that is *then* covered by white paint; white is not the colour *of* some underlying substance. Spaces are effected from the varying of some power – powers of colour, of texture, of line.

In the case of the literary work, Deleuze's references to both Virginia Woolf and D. H. Lawrence indicate that it is not modernist linguistic self-reflexivity that he draws upon but the attempt for language to no longer be propositional, no longer to be structured by a subject who judges the world to have this or that property. Instead, language would strive for affect – to release the powers or potential from which predication emerges. Language must somehow become a genuine *sign*, be *more* than the conventional relations of communication, and must open out to those sensations that may be liberated from any single perceiver or location.[30] Art, therefore, is not a return, nor a retrieval of the origin of form and meaning. This is where Deleuze's language of territorialization overturns any simple temporal recovery in the work of art; art is not, as it was for Heidegger, a way of attending to the experiential opening or forming of the world which has since been forgotten. For Deleuze, our actual world is a 'territory'; we speak and see according to habitual relations of recognition. We tie what we say to what we encounter in terms of our own regular and self-perpetuating rhythms.

The proposition is aligned with the subject in two senses: we see the world as a subject (a neutral x) which we can then predicate in various ways ('s is p'); but we *are* subjects insofar as we act as a stable viewpoint that predicates its world, referring one visual experience to another by virtue of shared and comparable qualities or predicates. We do not live the world as full, unmediated and impersonal chaos; we live only insofar as we orient our way in chaos. But Deleuze stresses the capacity for art, science and philosophy – which all begin by extending the powers of temporalization and spatialization that orient our lives – to go beyond practical orientation to *thinking*. Philosophy creates concepts that allow us to think the orientation, map[31] or territorialization of our lives, not in our practical relation to the world, but orientation as such, pure relations of thought. If, for example, we get through life by likening one thing to another through time and space, philosophy can create concepts, such as 'identity', which allow us to think that process. For Deleuze we are only doing philosophy when we think such processes *as processes*. That is, we should not explain identity by saying simply that 'x is like y', but should strive to understand the movement of mind that can carry a quality, likeness or sense through time. Thinking (or philosophy, which is one style of thinking alongside art and science) breaks with practice and grasps the structure or form that makes a practice possible; we can liken one thing to another, for example, only if we have some power of sense, some capacity to think of any isolated experience in terms of what it might be in other variations. So, from habits and practice, philosophy opens us up to the virtual powers of thinking, what thought can do, its power for creating relations.

Opinion, by contrast, creates habitual relations between the lived world and our response; we see a courtroom drama and think 'justice'; we see a white Western face and think 'humanity'; we pass directly from sensations to generalities. Art *de*territorializes this link between image and opinion. The whiteness of the face, so central to the 'subject' of Hollywood cinema – the whiteness that is immediately generalized as the self or interiority – can become a sign of a ghastly or ghostly inhumanity. In David Lynch's *Lost Highway* an uncanny visitor enters a cocktail party, informing the central character that he is at that very time in the character's house; his face is painted white, thus presenting white both as a colour and as a mask. The visitor asks the central character to phone him, and, when he does, the same character that is standing silent is *also* at home answering the call. Not only does this scene give us a time-image – for the ghostly character is at once present at the party *and* at home answering the call from the cell phone – it also shifts the habitual associations of affect with percept. The whiteness of the face is inhuman, spectral and unreal, working against a century of cinematic art that selects from the plane of composition – the sensations and affects that make up our world – but recomposes those materials in a way that allows them to stand alone, to be liberated from their habitual and unthinking linkage.

When art selects from the plane of composition it can do so only because it no longer sees the world in terms of human opinion; it deterritorializes the images of opinion and then recomposes or give another order (reterritorializes) by invoking a plane of composition. The crucial point for Deleuze and Guattari is that this is a 'higher deterritorialization'. If we can shake colour from its opinionated regularity, recompose it on to a canvas, then we are given to think the powers of colour or sensation as such. We go from territory – white as human or as subjectivity, where affect is tied to opinion – to deterritorialization – white as colour, sensation – to *re*territorialization: white as composed, framed and laid out on a canvas (as in a Cy Twombly painting), or white as paint, mask, dissimulator (as in Lynch's *Lost Highway*). So, while all life is deterritorialization[32] – for we would not have thought of humanity as 'white' were it not for the power of taking a quality beyond its actual occurrence and granting it a general extension – a 'higher deterritorialization' can occur when art takes this power of extending a quality beyond any generality. White is no longer the sign or symbol of some thing but a perceptual power or potential from which a world of perceived things emerges. The infinite is the power of any quality, any sensation whatever, to be seen, to be actualized, *to become*:

> The composite sensation, made up of percepts and affects, deterritorializes the system of opinion that brought together dominant perceptions and affections within a natural, historical and social milieu. But the composite sensation is reterritorialized on the plane of composition, because it erects its houses there, because it appears there within interlocked frames or joined sections that surround its components; landscapes that have become pure percepts, and characters that have become pure affects. At the same time the plane of composition involves sensation in a higher deterritorialization, making it pass through a sort of deframing which opens it up and breaks it open onto an infinite cosmos. . . . Perhaps the

peculiarity of art is to pass through the finite in order to rediscover, to restore the infinite.[33]

Just as Deleuze in his cinema books analyses how concrete formal techniques enable new images and relations of thought, so Deleuze and Guattari in *What is Philosophy?* use their definition of art as the creation of affects and percepts to explore quite specific differences in art history. It is in this regard that they overcome the opposition between formalist and historicist approaches. They acknowledge that a work of art always emerges from a context, or historical and cultural set of conditions and relations; but they also insist that the work is neither reducible to those relations, nor is it best understood in terms of those relations. Art is necessarily the reconfiguration of relations, or the capacity to open a new world or context. Once again this is where Deleuze differs from vitalism, historicism or philosophies of life, for he is always insistent that there are certain events *of life* – such as the work of art – which transform and re-create the very potentiality of life. Art does not emerge from certain possibilities inherent in life – say, the possibility that we can speak, paint, sing or move; rather, certain works of art create possibilities. It may well be that we only really come to think because 'we' have – maybe haphazardly – created an artwork. Paint is thrown on a canvas; it is only then that 'we' might ask what this means, and in so doing create a subject who thinks artistically. For Deleuze, then, there is not a subject whose trajectory of life expresses itself in external creation. His expressionism is the reverse of this: there are expressions – events, connections, creations, conjunctions – and it is from this that points of relative subjective stability are effected. We become viewers and creators of art through certain chance encounters – such as a social milieu which develops technologies of literature, sculpture, painting or cinema. It is from this chance encounter – which did not exist as some necessary potential awaiting expression *in life* such that life merely unfolds already given possibilities – that art as a specific type of expression emerges. We do not exist as subjects who then express themselves; rather, life produces certain modes of expression such as painting, writing, speaking, moving, sculpting, building and dancing, and each style of expression produces its own subject. There is no unified life or subject prior to its specific expressions.

If there is in Deleuze's philosophy a tendency to account for the emergence of styles of thought from life, this is intensified in his collaboration with Guattari, whose career was dominated by practical problems of how the syntheses of desire might be reconfigured.[34] How is it that desiring life creates certain debilitating conjunctions, and how as an analyst might one deal with such lives without appealing to some ultimately normative or proper life? In their jointly authored works, the work of art was always crucial to discussions of the relations between desiring life and norms. As Deleuze and Guattari argued in *Anti-Oedipus*, if history has produced 'man' or the 'subject' as a particular image which has enslaved and subordinated life, art creates new identifications, new affects or *counter-actualizations* – such that the virtual tendencies that produced one image ('man') can be drawn upon to produce other images. In their discussion, in *What is Philosophy?* of a standard art-historical observation – the 'birth' of perspective – they make three crucial points which direct the history of art away from any notion of a simple emergence from human nature.

First, their discussion begins from the idea of art as dealing with a plane of composition: how do we orient ourselves in the chaotic affects that confront us, without merely repeating rigid and habitual clichés? In order to live we require some order, some minimal 'territorialization' or subjectivity, but we also need to have some degree of creation or newness. A living being that remained absolutely within itself with no stimulus or interaction would not be a *living* being, but a pure and absolute openness to *all* difference would not yield a living *being*, would not allow some minimally stable, identifiable form. Sensation, they argue, is *worked upon* in art; art, unlike everyday or practical perception, does not fold perception around an acting and interested body. The artist uses material – paint, canvas, clay, plaster, sounds, lines, words, rhythms – to *liberate sensation*: 'sensation belongs to a different order and possesses an existence in itself for as long as the material lasts'.[35]

Second, despite their emphasis on philosophy, art and science as having essentially different tendencies – such that we can discern in all the composites of art just what it is that makes art *art* – they also form a *history* of art. This is possibly the most complex aspect of their collaboration, and resonates with their history of political life in *Anti-Oedipus* and also in their final reflections on the 'brain' as attaining the power to overcome the 'humanity' that was produced from political relations. In the case of art history they do not describe a teleological development whereby there is a proper form (such as realist representation) towards which art progresses, with technique being a vehicle for an increasingly true vision of life. Nor, however, is history a random sequence of one form after another. Rather, history is a style of duration; each mutation opens further paths for change that may or may not be actualized. (There were chances, say, in the history of philosophy that were not taken – and this is why Deleuze goes back to writers like Spinoza and Leibniz to see if we might imagine philosophy differently.) The future is not arrived at by steps, but there is a qualitative irreversible movement, and 'progress' is just the struggle any tendency of life undergoes in its force of self-differentiation: 'If there is progress in art it is because art can live only by creating new percepts and affects as so many detours, returns, dividing lines, changes of level and scale.'[36] The future of art, then, cannot be anticipated with reference to some transcendent norm, such as the representation of reality which might finally be achieved in a perspectival realism; nor would a modernism that captured the structures of experience or an avant-garde that finally freed itself from all content to become purely self-reflexive be exemplary instances of art in general. Progress and futurity are the achievement of difference, the capacity for techniques to achieve maximum difference. We could, then, evaluate the modernity of any epoch – say, Bach's genius for the creation of invention *within* the rules of the baroque. And we could also assess new forms on their capacity for invention; the novel, for example, opened a history of stunning variation, while the verse epistle was a less motile literary genre. Le Corbusier opened a number of legacies and potentialities in modern architecture, while the impact of Bernard Tschumi has not yet resulted in the same diverse uptake, but may also hold futures and potentials not yet actualized. The task of the critic is, at least in part, the assessment or diagnosis of a work's potentialities. If art is different from the everyday perception that must take a snapshot of life and establish some external referential world that remains the same through time, it is because art is *counter-actualisation* – taking the *force* of perception from which we synthesised a common external world, and presenting it as sensation itself. The more art techniques vary, the more history is liberated from a supposed progressive victory of 'man' over reality; art might be seen to achieve an inhuman, posthuman or impersonal plane of composition.

Third, and most importantly, Deleuze and Guattari's discussion of one of the critical points of art history demonstrates how their commitment to a plane of composition works, and how art as composition *creates* relations (rather than being subordinate to some already existing norm of reality or expression). To begin with, Deleuze and Guattari argue that technical processes are subordinate to the plane of composition. Art is not the perfection of technique, for technique exists only to liberate a sensation that depends upon, but is not reducible to, material.[37] Once again we might note that this would seem to preclude certain dominant 'postmodern' projects that both reduce art to mere matter, or that abandon technique as any form that would mediate material. In order to outline the relation between the plane of technique and the plane of composition, Deleuze and Guattari insist that techniques of perspective are a different way of working with material. We could make a comparison here with Deleuze's history of time and space in his *Cinema* books and the reference to art history in *What is Philosophy?* In both cases a distinction is made between different ways of organizing or stabilizing chaos, so that we can say both that there are historical stages but that such stages are not just progressions of degree so much as dramatic shifts in the very style of relations that compose experience. Deleuze and Guattari's account of art before and after perspective does not suggest that perspective is discovered as some better and inevitable relation to true representation, but they do insist that certain changes in history are singular: not just one change among others, but changes that radically shift potentials for future change. They distinguish between an earlier art-historical stage of perspective, where canvases are drawn, and outline and colour are added; and all this is done in order to conceal the intensity of the materials themselves so that they might open up a transcendent world. The canvas is a background, and in other arts – such as music where sounds are organized according to tonal progressions – the materials serve to create the sensation of a certain space. Art is still, they insist, not representation or copying, but it does aim to create a sensation that is not that of the painting itself: 'Art thus enjoys a semblance of transcendence that is expressed not in a thing to be represented but in the paradigmatic character of projection and in the "symbolic" character of perspective.'[38] Later, however, the background is not simply there to be delineated and formed, but takes on a life of its own such that the 'architecture' of the work, or its relations, emerge from colour, sound, texture and the light of the work itself.[39] In the very simplest terms we could think of the difference between the way in which Renaissance painting uses materials to create the effect of various angles of light in a room, the shadows of light on a body, and the experience of textures or spatial depth in the background surrounding the delineated forms. By comparison a modern work of art does not use its material to create sensations – does not, say, compose a symphony with a resolution in C major to create an affect of affirmation – but works with sensation itself: 'In the second case it is no longer sensation that is realized in the material *but the material that passes into sensation.*'[40] The works of Pierre Boulez, for example, explore tonal colours in their interacting relations, and not – as in Beethoven – with the *idea* that double-reeded instruments create a pastoral affect, trombones a demonic affect. The key point is the use Deleuze and Guattari make of this difference. Not only do they reject the idea that art declines with this second stage because the materials, such as the thickness of paint, neither last (literally) nor secure the clarity and permanence of form; they also detail different relations produced between the work of art and its relation to sensation, its power to transform sensation: 'In the first case *sensation is realized in the material* and does not exist outside of this realization.'[41] At its simplest we might say that a perspectival painting of clear lines (like a realist novel with clear descriptions) creates its own world; it does not refer to some outside world but does nevertheless create a relation of sensation where sensation is *of* some thing, some depth. With this technical achievement art establishes transcendence or an outside from its own plane through its technical plane, but this created world is not the higher world or beyond of religion; indeed, art is directly opposed to that life-denying spiritualist tendency of negating this world: 'its sensory transcendence enters into a hidden or open opposition to the suprasensory transcendence of religion'.[42]

This tendency to produce its own depth or outside already offers some potential for art to take itself further. That is, if art is the power of materials or techniques to free sensation from representation – with representations subordinating sensations to nothing more than the signs of some 'beyond' – then this power is maximized when the material 'passes into sensation'. We could see everyday practical perception as reducing sensations to those that will represent an ordered, knowable, manageable and predictable world. When perspectival art creates other worlds and spaces, it already opens sensation beyond what is present to another symbolized sensation, such as the light that is presented as deflecting from the various surfaces of a still life, or sounds that open up a pastoral scene in Beethoven's sixth symphony. When art no longer uses material to create sensations but allows the material *itself* to stand out as sensation, then we extend even further the power of art to be distinct from sensation as the sensation *of* some being. To use Deleuze's phrase from *Difference and Repetition* we would pass from the sensibility of being to the being of the sensible. Technique is now directed towards composition itself, and the colours, lights, forms or lines of the artwork 'create a thickness independent of any perspective or depth'.[43] This thickness is not, or not only, literal – not just the depth of paint laid over paint, colour on colour – for it also creates a *virtual* dimension. This occurs when art loses all relation to representation and reference, when art manipulates materials *as sensations*. The power of paint may bring all the potentials of colour to light, so that we see not just this red here, but what red *as sensation* might do, red as an infinitive or a 'to red . . .': 'painting is thought: vision is through thought, and the eye thinks even more than it listens'.[44] If art is *thinking*, but a thinking different from the concepts of philosophy, it is not because it follows an external reality faithfully, not because it masters reality, but because – like life in its highest power – it opens up worlds: 'To think, then, is to create food for thought.'[45] We are given the world not as it is, nor even as it reflects or serves our interests, but in its potential for difference:

> Are there not as many planes or universes, authors, or even works? In fact, universes, from one art to another as much as one and the same art, may derive from one another, or enter into relations of capture and form constellations of universes, independently of any derivation, but also scattering themselves into nebulae or different stellar systems, in accordance with qualitative distances that are no longer those of space and time.[46]

The notion of a distance that is neither temporal nor spatial can perhaps best be understood if we look at the way Deleuze and Guattari argue that this 'thickness' defines all art, including literature and music:

> It is characteristic of modern literature for words and syntax to rise up into the plane of composition and hollow it out rather than carry out the operation of putting it into perspective. It is also characteristic of modern music to relinquish projection and

the perspectives that impose pitch, temperament, and chromaticism, so as to give the sonorous plane a singular thickness to which very diverse elements bear witness.[47]

There can only be specifically spatial arts – or even philosophy's planes of immanence – if there is a power to differ, a power to produce relations or unfold differences, including the differences of time, of space, of colour, of sound, of thinking and of movement.

Higher deterritorialization occurs, then, not just when we liberate the sensations that have been domesticated to a homogenized time – say, when red means 'stop' or yellow means 'jealousy' – and not just when such sensations become powers or potentials 'to red . . .', or 'to yellow . . .', or when colour as such is given in its own difference. Higher deterritorialization gives us sensible difference and difference *thought through sensation.* Art is *thinking*, a specific style of thinking in its production of difference in sensations, just as philosophy is thinking in its production of difference through concepts. We think and live differently after a genuine concept is created, just as we see differently – and perhaps think of seeing differently – after the event of a work of art.

CHAPTER 5

POLITICS AND THE ORIGIN OF MEANING

TRANSCENDING LIFE AND THE GENESIS OF SENSE

Deleuze's most significant achievement in his cinema books was the demonstration that the technical mutations of dynamic life – from the eye to the camera – created different styles, shapes and forms of thought. Deleuze's spatial language is, therefore, always more than a metaphor: the relations, movements, orientations and connections among bodies produce maps of thinking. By freeing images from the sensory apparatus of the human body, which is oriented towards the mastery and appropriation of an objectified world, the cinematic image opens a new distance in thought; it allows the actual, located and presented image to exist alongside its virtual, potential and eternal double. In *Difference and Repetition* Deleuze had already argued that philosophy had been dominated by an image of thought: the figure of the rational mind that synthesizes its received sensations to constitute a stable object, and that harmonizes its actions with the minds of others to become the 'man' of good sense and common sense. If we do *without* this organizing image and consider the syntheses of images in themselves then we may have to consider a discordant subject. There would not be a self *who thinks*, but a thinking that occurs as an unwilled event and that cannot be reduced to a single locus or genesis. The rational and imaginative syntheses would diverge; the world of art that we feel would not be reducible to the world of concepts that we think, and neither would accord directly with the world of science that we deploy functionally.

If we accept the possibility that thought varies according to the image it has of itself – that we think a certain way, today, because we have the image of the mind or brain as the locus of thinking – then we might also consider the possibility announced in *Difference and Repetition* of thought 'without an image'. This is approached quite specifically in the *Cinema* books, where images are liberated from a viewing subject. But a thought liberated from utility and the function of 'man' is explored much earlier in the monumental *Anti-Oedipus*, co-authored with Félix Guattari (published in French in 1972). We can get some idea of the audacity of this work by considering, first, what mutation occurred when Deleuze encountered Guattari and, second, the ways in which this encounter transformed the problematic terrain of twentieth-century thought.

Prior to *Anti-Oedipus* Deleuze had already explored the origin of meaning from both a phenomenological and psychoanalytic point of view, particularly in his *Logic of Sense* (published in French in 1969). Rather than simply accept that there are systems or structures of meaning that allow us to regard any present aspect of life as having a certain sense (and therefore as identifiable through time, beyond its present occurrence), Deleuze had outlined two geneses of sense. On the one hand, following phenomenology, sense relies on the event of the noematic attribute: we see not only this concrete perceived datum but see it *as* something, and thus perception is both oriented to seeing *something* (not just passively or blindly receiving) *and* is directed beyond the present to what maintains itself through time.[1] All these perceptions are perceptions *of* 'x', so the perceptual act – or noeisis – of seeing, imagining, remembering, anticipating, hallucinating, is accompanied by the perceived, or the noema – that which is seen, remembered, imagined and so on. This means that all experience, to draw upon phenomenology, is *intentional*, or directed beyond itself to what is not itself, what transcends or is transcendent. Deleuze's philosophy was always to maintain this aspect of phenomenology; he did not simply accept a transcendent or 'outside' world, but asked how transcendence was constituted. He disagreed with phenomenology's argument that *consciousness* constituted its world, but he maintained the argument originally articulated by Husserl that transcendence emerges from immanence; the differentiation between inside and outside, between self and world, between the experienced lived world of sense and the world lived, emerges from dynamic life, and should not be accepted as some original difference which might explain life. We should not, therefore, consider the world only as it is lived, sensed or experienced, for we have to account for how these relations of experience emerge.

For Deleuze, particularly in *The Logic of Sense*, sense or the milieu through which the difference between the world as it is actually and the world as it is perceived or sensed cannot be explained by consciousness. Deleuze refers to the problem, here, of 'static genesis'. We should look at any philosophy, such as a philosophy that explains experience, by referring to two terms (say, mind and sense data) and then ask how that image of mind as opposed to data is structured or related. Deleuze will respond by saying that such relations are only possible because of a paradoxical or aleatory element.[2] Consider, for example, the consciousness that supposedly explains how any world is possible: we can only have a world because there is some consciousness that connects experiences through time and produces a coherent series of perceptions as this lived and meaningful world; at the same time, though, consciousness is also lived as a part of this world, as experienced. Sense, Deleuze argues, is just this surface that allows us to imagine a world on the one hand and an experiencing mind on the other; such binaries or schemas are produced through particular distributions of sense, but if we tried to say or articulate that schema we would be producing yet one more sense, never the origin of sense itself. There is always a surface between the world lived and the life that lives, and if we try to understand this surface we will always be *making sense of life*; we cannot, therefore *say* the sense of sense.

In addition to this static genesis, which argues that any schema accounting for the possibility of experience has to be generated from at least one term that is itself never fully accountable within experience, Deleuze also refers to 'dynamic genesis'. How is the noematic surface of sense effected, the surface that produces experience as the experience *of* this or that thing? Deleuze, in *The Logic of Sense*, follows both Melanie Klein and Jacques Lacan. From partial objects or the body's tendency to privilege the connection of certain parts – mouth to breast, caressing hand to arm – a good object is produced as an image of integrity, an initial wholeness or identity, something that *is*. This first stage of partial objects is not, yet, lived as a unified world set over against a self-identical subject. The 'I' who speaks and represents a world that is lived as coherent and objective is given only through the oedipal structure. This occurs when the phallus becomes that virtual body part that appears as the figure of an order or law.[3] Phenomenology had already linked sense to a world of other subjects: to live this world as being the same through time and as real is also to live it as there for others, as intersubjective. To see this experience as the experience *of* some objective meaningful thing – as having sense – is already to imply a world or milieu beyond my immediate perceptions and affects. The Oedipus complex is a way of explaining the emergence, or dynamic genesis, of this lawful world. *Sense* – the idea of an order to which bodies are subject – appears first as the aleatory or paradoxical object of the phallus; for the phallus is not a body part that has meaning, so much as an element that signals *that there is meaning*, that the mixture of bodies and relations is supervened by a surface of sense that is not just what I see here and now but is also a world for others and for all time. Lacan explains how the phallus becomes the privileged virtual object through the figure of sexual difference: the first relation to the other's body is to the body of the mother, with separation from that maternal body occurring in the subjection to symbolization. The speaking subject is therefore 'he' who must accept the law of the symbolic order; he *is* only insofar as he speaks within that structure; there can be no 'I' who is not an 'I' speaking within the law. Woman, by contrast, is that which has been abandoned for the sake of the law, and so she is that which lacks the law (the phallus being the sign of this lack, the lack of sense).[4]

Up until this point of his work, Deleuze is in accord, for the most part, with the tendencies of Lacanian psychoanalysis and poststructuralism. The clearest achievement of the Lacanian corpus lay in the idea that the signifier is tied to an oedipal fantasy of lack.[5] From a *corporeal* relation – the body's need for food, the mouth's connection to the breast – an image of another body orients desire. The other's body that offers food – a body of partial objects of breast, mouth, hand and so on – becomes a speaking body, a mouth that speaks, only when needs (the instincts of the body) become demands (drives directed to this other who must answer my need, whose desire I must address).[6] Desire is just this subjection of need to another's body whose own needs are not present, whose image or sense of the world is *not given*. Relations among bodies are subjected to the system of signification, a system that is never given in full but only figured through the image of the law: *that there is sense*. For we can never say sense itself; desire always passes through the system of signification, is never at one with itself, and is therefore compelled to for ever circle around a presence it must presuppose but never achieve. Lacan therefore offers the oedipal scene as the fantasy that subtends sense: we are submitted to signification and we live that submission to signification as a trauma or wound inflicted on our being, imagining both a full enjoyment that is deferred (an object not submitted to system, a woman or 'beyond'), and an Other or law who prohibits that beyond. Sexual difference is a logic or fantasmatic formula that structures the way we live this world as *being*, as existing not just for me but for others, and therefore as lawful and objective.

Poststructuralism, particularly in its Derridean form, appeared to offer a counter-argument to the Lacanian oedipal scene. How, Derrida argued, can psychoanalysis explain the emergence of sense, the emergence of difference *and* the fantasy of this scene? To do so it would have to command or purvey the system of differences. But, as Derrida argues, psychoanalysis is itself already a scene and a text. It cannot therefore be the story of all stories, the truth of all truths. Psychoanalysis's attempt to demystify the oedipal fantasy, by arguing that we live our own subjection to system through the figure of a lost plenitude and an intervening law, must itself employ an imaginary figure of mastery: the analyst who confronts system itself, the pure signifier, without the illusion of meaning, truth or presence. This image of mastery creates a fantasy of the truth of truth, or ultimate presence.[7]

This impasse between psychoanalysis and poststructuralism would seem to be final. Either we work through and traverse our fantasies of sense by reading all culture and writing as an attempt to make sense of the absence of ultimate presence, or we abandon any attempt to *master* a scene and attend to the scriptural or textual mechanisms that open a scene. Consider, for example, two styles of reading epitomized in the 1980s debate regarding Lacan's reading of Edgar Allan Poe.[8] Lacan had read 'The Purloined Letter' as a fantasmatic scene. A letter implicating the Queen in an affair is stolen by a government minister. The Queen asks a detective, Dupin, to retrieve the letter, and the detective does so – *not* by searching the minister's apartment meticulously (as the police had done) but by reading the minister's desire. The detective Dupin imagines where one might place a letter if one considered oneself to be the master of a situation. The detective knows that the minister considers himself to be cleverer than the police, and so the minister will place the letter where he knows the police will not look for it – out in the open, on display on the mantelpiece. Lacan draws several conclusions from this story. First, it is not the *content* of the letter that is important (not what it means) but its position (who holds the letter, who is deemed to hold the letter). It is not *what* something means so much as the fact that one looks for meaning, that one searches for what is not given. Second, our relations to the *letter* are determined by reading other subject's desires: not, 'what does the letter mean?', but 'how does the other person read my relation to the letter?' The master of Poe's story – the detective – does not look for the letter itself, but thinks of where it would be *for others*. Finally, the letter strictly speaking is nothing in itself. All the characters and positions are determined by how they imagine others will act; the letter remains, in itself, devoid of force. In reading the story, Lacan regarded the text as displaying the truth of human relations to the signifier.[9]

By contrast, Derrida responded to the Lacanian reading by taking the supposed dominance of the signifier as insurmountable. One could not read the story as an *example* or privileged allegory of the way in which subjects relate to each other through signification, for the story is itself a text and is produced through signifiers that cannot be mastered. In all his readings, therefore, Derrida looks at the concrete textual traces from which any scene is opened, including the psychoanalytic scene that would explain Poe's story as offering *the* truth of truth. In Poe's story, for example, a narrative voice places the story in a scene and thereby indicates that 'before' there can be a play among subjects there must be a marking that produces subject positions. The 'I' who narrates Poe's story, for example, creates a space outside the scene narrated, a point of view from which the characters – including the detective Dupin – might be observed. It is this 'scene of writing', a scene that one can never step outside or master, that Lacan fails to consider. Lacan does not, and cannot, account for how his own position of mastery is generated.

This simple acceptance of *a* position in command of truth, and of psychoanalysis as a master narrative, will receive stringent criticism in Deleuze and Guattari's *Anti-Oedipus*: yes, they concede, we may all be subjected to the fantasy of the Other, or father-figure, who holds the truth of our being, but we need to account for the historical and political genesis of this fantasy.[10] Whereas Deleuze and Guattari will trace the historical emergence of the seemingly inescapable and universal system of signification, and Deleuze will always insist on tracing the genesis of signs from life, Derrida will insist that we are always within differential relations, never able to position ourselves in a position of knowledge beyond difference; there is no pure outside of the text.[11] In contrast to a reading method that interprets texts according to a privileged oedipal scene or a supposed imaginary through which 'we' live our subjection to system, deconstruction exposes the impossibility of system. On the one hand, experience only has sense if it is oriented to revealing some presence, if it is directed beyond itself to something that *is*. Experience is oriented to what is not given. On the other hand, this presence or full givenness can never arrive, never release itself from the differential movement from which it is effected. Deconstructive readings, therefore, affirm a differential movement 'before' any imaginary scene (and 'before' any 'before' and 'after', any narrative, or any subject).[12]

We seem to be caught between two tendencies: the recognition that our submission to structure is imagined through some primal scene of sense (a fantasized enjoyment we demand but can never fulfil), *or* the affirmation of this systemic dispersal by a deconstruction that affirms play and refuses all nostalgia or mastery.

BEYOND THE SYMBOLIC AND IMAGINARY

Deleuze's early work was already at odds with both the deconstructive and Lacanian tendencies. Even though he had described the emergence of sense through an oedipal scene (in *The Logic of Sense and Difference and Repetition*), the dominant project of his work was the liberation of thought from its organizing images. Indeed, despite the fact that many writers following Deleuze today have turned back to the biological and physical theories that underpin his philosophy, Deleuze's project has always distinguished between the emergence of a phenomena and its potentials for divergence. This project was articulated explicitly in *Difference and Repetition* with the posited goal of 'thought without an image' but was also in the background of his readings of Bergson, Hume and Spinoza: philosophers who studied the syntheses of thought to explain and overcome its internal tendencies towards illusion. In his later encounter with Guattari, Deleuze both politicizes the twentieth-century obsession with the signifier and confronts the theoretical paradigm of Lacanian psychoanalysis.[13] If we look at Guattari's work we can discern certain themes – the machine, transversality and schizoanalysis – that enabled *Deleuze* and Guattari to create a history of the dominant image of thought.[14] Deleuze's philosophical problem – the ways in which the differential movements, connections and flows of life (or syntheses) had been organized by a central image of thought – became a manifestly political problem: how had desire or the flow of life come to see itself, imagine itself, as desire *for* a lost, impossible, fantasmatic object, a presence mediated by a signifier? Put *politically*: how can we explain the individual's desire for fascism without appealing to some natural concept of the self which is then accidentally corrupted? The remarkable achievement of *Anti-Oedipus* is that this question is answered in a seemingly simple manner: capitalism.[15]

But Deleuze and Guattari's overcoming of *oedipal* psychoanalysis – a psychoanalysis that assumes that desire takes the form of a familial fantasy – does not assume a Marxist narrative whereby the bourgeois family is located within a history of other familial forms. Far more radically, Deleuze and Guattari write a history of personhood as such, and tie this history to a capitalism that is not just one economic form among others but a tendency of all life, a tendency towards exchange and the creation of surplus. Capitalism in the narrow sense is the domination, by money, of a more general and open network of exchange. The realizations of capitalism *and* the Oedipus complex are contingent, but once they do emerge they enable a reading of life as such. Deleuze and Guattari do not just *oppose* Lacanian psychoanalysis or poststructuralism; they argue that both movements are accurate up to a point. But how, they ask, is it possible that 'man' has become capable of recognizing himself as a desiring being whose relations are submitted to a law of 'the' signifier? And how has writing – the system of difference as such – come to overcode *all* the flows of life? Why is it that we see all relations as mediated by textuality, or that we regard the world as knowable only though discourse? Capitalism, Deleuze and Guattari argue, is the conjunction in history of certain tendencies of life, the tendency for desire to liberate itself from its originally formed relations (deterritorialization), along with the tendency to re-form new systems of relations (reterritorialization).

When Deleuze and Guattari write a *history* of flows they do not allow one epoch to follow another as so many discrete changes or progressions – from primitivism to feudalism to capitalism. Rather, such epochs are realizations of a potential in life, a potential that always remains or 'haunts' various forms. Capitalism was a potential that was 'warded off' by primitive and barbaric societies, with the despot acting to control the flows of objects. Similarly, there are primitive and barbaric archaisms in capitalist culture, revealed in despotic fantasies. Deleuze and Guattari's history takes the form of a *duration*, rather than a series of discrete points; the potentials for life to flow or become alter with each contingent encounter. If capitalism and bourgeois 'man' come to appear as the truth and essence of our being, and as historically destined, this is because there is a potential in life to produce such forms, such that they cannot be lamented as intrusions on an otherwise communal life. But such forms also enable their own critique, and it is just this contingent emergence of the capacity to *read* and discern capital that Deleuze and Guattari wish to intuit. Deleuze and Guattari do not just write *Anti-Oedipus* from some elevated position beyond life and capital; they explain how the flows of life lead *both* to capitalism *and* its immanent critique. They account for the emergence of their own historical position, how capitalism and oedipal man enable their own overcoming.

SHIT AND MONEY

To begin to make this clear we can consider two of the 'flows' examined in *Anti-Oedipus*: shit and money. Deleuze's later reflection on money in his *Cinema* books describes cinema's confrontation with money. Whereas the essence or tendency of cinema is its potential to open the actual world by allowing its virtual potential to appear, money is, by contrast, a mechanism for rendering the fluidity and becoming of life axiomatic.[16] In *Anti-Oedipus* Deleuze and Guattari make this axiomatic of money more cogent by contesting both the structuralist and capitalist assumptions that human life is inaugurated in exchange. Here, their history both of money and of shit becomes important. Money is ultimately what allows for privatization, such that human relations are no longer governed by an external authority (the despot), nor a collective investment (where the desire of bodies is directed towards a certain intensity or flow of life – all the bodies of the tribe assembling through flows of sound, or pain). The first privatization, they argue, occurs with the anus. Here we have to pause and note that to a certain extent Deleuze and Guattari's account of the genesis of 'man', writing, civilization and money is mythic – a story told after the event, from the relations of the present. It is a 'geology' or an attempt to discern how the relations of the present have been distributed. Their myth is, however, an active method of intuiting *from capitalist bourgeois humanism* the forces and events that allowed for its emergence. And this assumes that the past remains present, virtually, in the fantasies, memories and relations that can resurface with the appropriate concentration or analysis. Their history is a geography of life, a dissection of the forces that compose the current terrain. Privatization may be the motor force of contemporary capital and the structure of oedipal man, but it is heralded in what Deleuze and Guattari refer to as the primitive socius.[17]

Desire, they insist, does not begin as the desire of a private subject who can then enter the marketplace and negotiate with others how to achieve his outcomes. Desire is collective and intensive, so that one can imagine a group of bodies – the primitive socius – as one desiring flow, such that desire's *investments*, or the impassioned and intense elevation of a body part, create a social group: the eyes all directing their vision towards this image; or the bodies all moving, flowing, towards the joyous destruction of this animal; or the limbs all moving, flowing in concert, to this rhythm. The bodies assembled around the primitive phallus create a territory, with the 'social machine' being the *recording* of desire, its stabilization or inscription in a relatively fixed form. All desire is productive insofar as it creates relations and produces territories. Desiring machines are coupled with social machines that effect a certain anti-production or a tendency to take the active and dynamic flows of desire in order to form a static or regular inscription of their movement.[18] In its filial form, for example, the social machine takes the events of human history and becoming and records and inscribes these movements as the history *of humanity* – a history of successive and progressive generations of the same unit ('man'). In so doing, this recording which appears to *add* a regular schema to events also lessens their original force: human bodies are desiring and productive, but if their desire and production come to be regulated by some form or system then an element of that desire is directed or deflected by the social totality. The collective investments of the primitive socius do not allow for a heavily coded social machine, but there is a movement towards coding or a tendency for movements and relations to be subjected to a single unit.[19]

In order to write a history of money and its connection with the private familial 'man' of the Oedipus complex, Deleuze and Guattari focus on three features of potential life: before there is exchange there is the *gift* and *theft*; before there is private 'man' there is collective investment and group fantasy; and before there are relations and systems of persons there is an 'intense germinal influx', a life irreducible to its mediated forms. It is this latter potential for *intensity* that allows Deleuze and Guattari, in *Anti-Oedipus* and *A Thousand Plateaus*, to criticize the current dominance of writing and signification. We can deal with these three potentialities in turn.

EXCHANGE, GIFT AND THEFT

Deleuze and Guattari's argument regarding the gift and theft also charts the emergence of debt, a debt that in modern humanism becomes private, internal and infinite. The twentieth-century structuralist anthropologist Claude Lévi-Strauss had argued that culture is predicated upon exchange; we abandon the immediacy of mere life and enter into relations with others. In arguing this he perpetuated a primarily utilitarian concept of human life: human beings depart from animality and immediate desire for the sake of some higher end. So, rather than remain within one's immediate family, and rather than remain immediately gratified with mere animal life, human's prohibit incest and allow marriage only with other families; it is this prohibition that propels human life into negotiation and exchange with others. Women therefore become objects of exchange, and social relations are effected from the requirement to look beyond one's own family for sexual gratification. In this kinship exchange one must recognize others as having a right to a pleasure one has denied oneself; but this sacrifice of one's own enjoyment is counteracted by reciprocity, for one can enjoy the other tribe's women. On this structuralist account, humans defer immediate needs and in so doing mediate their desires through negotiation with others. It is through this mediation or deferral through exchange that culture is inaugurated. Although Lévi-Strauss's work appeared to be radical in its description of culture as having no specific content and appearing only as the negation and structuration of nature, it also drew upon late nineteenth-century assumptions regarding the emergence of 'man' from 'life'. According to Michel Foucault, it was in the eighteenth century that 'man' came to be understood as a being who is produced precisely because the needs of life require negotiation, systematization and management. Foucault therefore argued that structuralism, which looked like an overcoming of humanism and its specific norms and values, nevertheless committed itself to an image of life which required some universal structuration; indeed, 'man' in his modern form differs from earlier humanism in that he has no specific character or essence other than his relation to a life that he must master and mediate, a life that was the hidden force behind the structures of language, society and labour.[20] Lévi-Strauss's structuralism was, therefore, similar in motivation to psychoanalysis, phenomenology, and certain forms of Marxism and existentialism; all these movements depicted 'man' as the being who is *other than mere* life, whose desire for what is not immediate and present separates him from all positive being and compels him to enter some structure of deferral of present desire for the sake of an anticipated and collectively recognized human end. Hegel, who had argued that consciousness emerges through negation, or the capacity for humans to act for the sake of what is not given or immediate, was – for both Deleuze and Foucault – *the* figure in the history of philosophy who had installed lack, negation and mediation at the heart of thinking. The figure of exchange that dominated Lévi-Strauss's anthropology was, therefore, far from being a radical break with earlier normative images of life, for in all cases it was assumed that human beings use exchange or relations to create some form of social equilibrium: we sacrifice immediate desire, but in so doing secure a more stable, continuous and meaningful life. That is, 'man' delays his immediate needs but in so doing allows those needs to be met more effectively and efficiently. We thereby move from the chaotic and haphazard world of animal life to the managed and predictable world of human life, from a chaotic and directionless time of mere chance to a measured and calculated social time. In the case of exchange, for example, we work more than is required by simple need, or we deny the desire for those bodies immediately present to us – we detach ourselves from mere life – but this then allows us to live our lives with greater efficiency; our extra work produces a surplus that can be exchanged and that can yield even further production, and our deferred desire leads to marriages and kinship structures that allow for social stability.

Against this privileging of exchange Deleuze and Guattari draw upon Marcel Mauss and Nietzsche to argue for a disequilibrium of theft and gift. In the case of theft, they draw upon Nietzsche, Georges Bataille and Jean Genet: we can imagine a force of so much power that, rather than aiming to preserve or maintain itself – rather than submit to maintaining a stable force – has the energy to expend itself violently and thoughtlessly, without attention to worth, production or maintenance. In the case of the gift, they draw upon Marcel Mauss, who insists that human life is not defined by functional exchange, where we give up so much energy only because we anticipate some sort of profit or return that will stabilize and maintain life. Rather, the gift is the spending of energy *not* for the sake of return; indeed, one's force is increased the more one spends. (Think of how much power is gained, for example, by a sovereign who wastes forces lavishly in display and festival, and who appears to do so without any regard for recognition; and think, by contrast, how capitalist uses of the gift industry, from Valentine's Day to Christmas, actually negate this potentiality to give without return or recognition.) Is human potentiality, Deleuze and Guattari ask, really disclosed in the systems of negotiation that serve life and the maintenance of sameness and equilibrium, where 'we' all recognize each other as equivalent? Or is desire not better revealed in a surpassing or excess of life?

At the heart of this question is Deleuze's philosophical commitment to understanding what something is, not by looking at its common, repeatable or usual manifestation – the general – but by asking what something *might be* if its tendencies were pushed to the extreme. Thus, we understand cinema not by looking at what films are usually like, but by asking what it is that cinema *can do*, the cinematic powers that are different from novels or scientific treatises. And we ask what philosophy is, not by looking at what features all the works of philosophy share – again a generalization – but by asking what powers of thinking enable all these different and disparate manifestations: what must thinking be capable of if there is something like philosophy? In the case of *Anti-Oedipus* Deleuze and Guattari refuse to begin their explanation of desire from what 'man' currently appears to be; instead they ask what historical forces produced contemporary oedipal man, and how those forces might be extended *beyond man*.

Deleuze and Guattari's history of life in *Anti-Oedipus* describes the ways in which the flows of life are subsumed by capital and exchange. In its final form 'man' becomes a labouring being whose force is no longer invested in a *coded* flow, directed to a specific object such as the divine earth or terrifying despot, but is decoded and deterritorialized through money and labour. Money, which begins initially as a way of *coding* exchange (so that I can represent two non-equivalent products in terms of some external value), becomes in capitalism a form of decoding: the flow of money itself is desired and is no longer a quantity of some abstracted labour value. Concurrently, labour is also deterritorialized. At its simplest, producing bodies are no longer located and inscribed through their producing identity, where what one does coincides with social function and position. Labour is a force put to any use whatever, becoming a stock. (Think of the way, today, that labour functions can migrate across the globe, with call centres shifting services offshore, and the way that labouring bodies can also move fluidly, with immigrant workers being used as so much force for whatever labour happens to be required at the time.[21]) Crucially, capital, which was once a flow of *alliance* – allowing relations among groups and bodies, becomes *filiative*: capital appears as the origin or ground from which all relations emanate. We explain all culture, for example, as emerging from the submission to systems of exchange. It is this distinction and history of alliance and filiation that Deleuze and Guattari employ to criticize both the dominance of exchange, and the image of private familial man who is submitted to the empty structures of a world that is nothing more than a conjunction of flows of money and labour.

Deleuze and Guattari structure *Anti-Oedipus* around three broad historical epochs and three syntheses. The attention paid to synthesis has a complex philosophical and political heritage. It not only recalls (as in Deleuze's early work on Kant and Hume) the ways in which the mind connects images to form unities;[22] it also refers to social connections, and it is significant that in *Anti-Oedipus* Deleuze and Guattari make no clear distinction between social syntheses and the syntheses of the mind. The first synthesis is that of production, so that life, *or life as desire*, is productive. Here, we already encounter a challenge to the exchangist model. Desire, Deleuze and Guattari argue, is not a relation *from* one body to another; nor is it the striving for what one body does not have:

> Desire is the set of *passive syntheses* that engineer partial objects, flows, and bodies, and that function as units of production. The real is the end product, the result of the passive syntheses of desire as autoproduction of the unconscious. Desire does not lack anything; it does not lack its object. It is, rather, the *subject* that is missing in desire, or desire that lacks a fixed subject; there is no fixed subject unless there is a repression. Desire and its object are one and the same thing: the machine, as a machine of a machine.[23]

Desire is the production, from flows or connections, of bodies as relatively stable points. If we go back to the classic psychoanalytic paradigm, Deleuze and Guattari contest the image of a child whose need would place it in a position of dependence and demand in relation to its mother. Rather, they begin from the image of flows – flows of milk from breast to mouth, flows of faeces from the anus, flows of looks from the face, flows of touches from hands to limbs, connections of lips to food or breast or hand – and these couplings and connections produce 'desiring machines' which might then be coded or inscribed *as* mother and child. Before the relation of desire between two terms, then, there are flows that produce relatively stable terms and certain styles of relation or synthesis. It is illegitimate to begin explanation from relations between terms because terms are initially effected or produced *not* from extended units – mother or child – but from *intensities*, a flowing towards that which will enhance or expand not life as it is but life as it might become. A desire directed towards an extended object is the desire for this or that repeatable and recognizable thing; but such a desire is only possible because of an intensity: the desire of mouth that is drawn to the breast not to refind what it has lost but to push further and further into connecting, touching, sucking, consuming.

The second synthesis, the disjunctive synthesis, creates relations, so that a flow (or machine) produced from the first connective synthesis – say, mouth to breast – oscillates around points of relative stability; the mouth can select breast *or* food *or* finger *or* noise. The problem comes in, Deleuze and Guattari argue, when these syntheses effected *from life* (and which are therefore immanent) come to appear as laws to which life ought to submit. The entire methodology of both *Anti-Oedipus* and *A Thousand Plateaus* lies in the distinction between immanent and transcendent syntheses, with the former being produced from the flows of life, while the latter is taken to be some system of laws or relations which would govern life. So, on an immanent understanding, the connections of life produce a harmony of accords, some flows producing expansive connections that create further connections and further flows, and a harmony of discords, where certain connections produce little or no resonance. On a transcendent understanding the harmony of life would be some pre-established order. And it is just this transcendent understanding of synthesis that Deleuze criticizes in Kant, who argues that experience is only possible if it obeys three lawful syntheses:

a coherent succession (first synthesis), a capacity to place that succession in terms of a before and after (second synthesis), and then the attribution of all those successive and temporally ordered experiences to the point of view of a subject who experiences. For Deleuze, by contrast, it is precisely the power of life to connect *beyond* coherence and comprehension that is significant.

The task of *Anti-Oedipus* is therefore to see syntheses in their revolutionary power, their power to go beyond recognition and coherence. In the case of the disjunctive synthesis, which is produced from a movement around relatively stable points – one can be this *or* this *or* this – we can see its illegitimate or transcendent use in the principle of exchange: either you desire your mother and remain in pre-oedipal chaos *or* you identify with your father and submit to the rules of culture. Such a disjunction is restrictive rather than inclusive. And this illusion, which takes the social inscription of desire for desire itself, also loses sight of desire's excessive force. The idea of exchange begins from a notion of *extended* alliance: there are bodies – of mother, father, child – that enter into lateral relations with other bodies (other families) and thus produce culture as a stable network of exchange. Such an account would also privilege a notion of *debt*, so that each sexual relation requires *in return* another body. In the pre-modern stages of history, according to Deleuze and Guattari, such debt is finite and applied to a specific term: one pays another tribe with women. In capitalism the debt becomes infinite because one is submitted to a law and system, but this law does not demand a particular body so much as empty and formal submission. Culture explained in terms of exchange therefore begins with specific bodies – men, women, fathers, mothers – but does not ask about the genesis of these identities. How have these extended bodies been produced? Here, Deleuze and Guattari refer to the significance of the gift and to filiation. Whereas alliance relates groups of bodies horizontally or laterally to each other, and is therefore a spatial concept, filiation relates bodies to their origins and descendants and is a temporal notion: relations between tribes are relations of alliance, but the emergence of the child as son or daughter from the mother or father is a relation of filiation.

One of Deleuze and Guattari's most complex terms, the 'body without organs', is produced from their understanding of an intense and original filiation, whereby the desires of the bodies on the primitive socius bear a filiative relation to the mythic earth. Bodies are not yet organized into interchangeable units that can be exchanged (such as mothers and sisters from one family to another). Deleuze and Guattari posit an 'intense germinal influx' where bodies are not yet differentiated into coded forms – mother, father, child – but are intensively different:

> It is the great nocturnal memory of the intensive germinal filiation that is repressed for the sake of an extensive somatic memory, created from filiations that have become extended (patrilineal *or* matrilineal) and from the alliances that they imply . . .
>
> The system in extension is born of the intensive conditions that make it possible, but it reacts on them, cancels them, represses them, and allows them no more than a mythical expression. The signs cease to be ambiguous at the same time as they are determined in relation to the extended filiations and the lateral alliances: the disjunctions become exclusive, restrictive (the 'either/or else' replaces the intense 'either . . . or . . . or . . .'); the names, the appellations no longer designate intensive states, but discernible persons.[24]

That is, in their broader understanding of life, which becomes more apparent in *A Thousand Plateaus*, desiring life is intensive difference. A body is made up of powers to differ, and these powers are actualized in productive encounters. A child becomes a child when its body encounters a breast that is a part-object of a 'mother' who only has *this* identity because she, in turn, is connected to a social field. And motherhood, like all other personal images, is directly political: there are mothers because of social relations and images. The condition for these social relations is an intensive life that *exceeds* the relations it produces. There is, in life, a potentiality for mother–child organizations, but such potentials might have been actualized in different relations. In the case of same-sex female couples with children, for example, it might be difficult to align one body directly or exclusively with the relation of mother. This desiring intensity of life is perhaps best understood as sexual difference: not the difference *between* two sexes, but a flow of desiring difference where each connection of body to body creates a relation and pairing of terms. It is the social familial relation, for example, that produces certain women as mothers; and on such an understanding lesbians would not be women precisely because 'woman' is defined as one who relates in a binary to man.[25]

When Deleuze and Guattari emphasize the potential of 'becoming-woman' they therefore open the seemingly self-evident sexual binary to the differential processes from which that binary is effected.[26] Sexual difference is not the result of a division of bodies into male and female. Rather, all life is sexual difference – a power of life to connect and create desiring relations or 'desiring machines'. The male–female dyad is one production, but one could (and should) imagine other productions. So, rather than seeing woman as the object that is first prohibited and then exchanged, where all desire would be *for* that lost object, one needs to see desire as *more* than any of its effected connections.

The child's desire opens out on to a diverse field, and should not be seen as originally directed to the maternal origin:

> It is strange that we had to wait for the dreams of colonized peoples to see that, on the vertices of the pseudo triangle, mommy was dancing with the missionary, daddy was being fucked by the tax collector, while the self was being beaten by a white man. It is precisely this pairing of the parental figures with another nature, their locking embrace similar to that of wrestlers, that keeps the triangle from closing up again, from being valid in itself, and from claiming to express or represent this different nature of the agents that are in question in the unconscious itself.
>
> . . . The father, the mother, and the self are at grips with, and directly coupled to, the elements of the political and historical situation – the soldier, the cop, the occupier, the collaborator, the radical, the resister, the boss, the boss's wife – who constantly break all the triangulations, and who prevent the entire situation from falling back on the familial complex and becoming internalized in it.[27]

Deleuze and Guattari are highly critical of the contemporary psychoanalysis that 'reads' the child's connections with all sorts of machines as *really* a signification of its desire for the mother. In historical terms they describe a primitive socius where collective desire produces relations by connecting body parts, animal intensities and images of the divine earth. Such *intensities* or relations of desire precede the *extended* bodies or terms of mother–father–child of the modern family. Before there are extended relations among terms (alliance and exchange) there must be a surplus or excess of desire.

Desire does not remain within itself but branches out to connect with other desires. The condition for the calculation, exchange and self-interest that maintains any body in a relatively stable state through time is an *excessive expenditure*. Once again, we can define such excessive expenditure as sexual difference. If organisms were solely directed towards self-maintenance then they would only act or expend energy for the sake of reproduction, but sexuality as such is a relation to other bodies without anticipation of production or return. As Freud details in his *Three Essays on Sexuality*, the infant that sucks on the breast for nourishment maintains its life, but when the sucking itself becomes sensual and enjoyable – regardless of nourishment – then we attain the sexual itself *as surplus*.[28] This insistence on life as potentiality for excess rather than stability and equilibrium is evidenced in a historical tendency towards what Deleuze and Guattari refer to as a 'surplus value of code'. It is not by prohibition or restriction that social machines emerge, but by consumption. The despot who consumes *more* than his share is one instance of a power of life to exceed that which is prudently required for life; the desire to consume to excess goes beyond self-maintenance and produces points of relative stability. In such cases, power can be maximized by excessive consumption, with the despot achieving power by seizing the surplus of society's productions; but history is also replete with despots who have destroyed themselves in excessive consumption, who *rather than maintain their position of power* enjoy an abundance of life to the point of self-destruction. We could even imagine that early capitalism's refusal to allow for excess, where all surplus is redirected towards creating more and more production, could, if pushed to its limit, tip the system into crisis. However, as has occurred in late capitalism, excessive consumption has itself become part of the flow of production; the useless and seemingly unproductive expenditure of fashion, novelty, leisure, and even the commodification of sexual perversion by the sex industry, has returned all abandonment and disregard for self-maintenance to the maintenance of the capitalist system.[29] So, the power of capitalism does not lie in its repression of our pleasures, but in its coding of all those pleasures into money *and* in producing a surplus value of that code: for we are now enslaved, not by being *denied what we want*, but by being manufactured *to want*. My desire must be *for* this or that purchasable pleasure. Capitalism can only remain stable if the surplus that is seized from production to enhance the capitalist machine is balanced by some expenditure or enjoyment, but it is possible that the increasing alignment of any enjoyment with production – where all our contemporary pleasures serve the market and exchange – could bring about a revolutionary collapse of the system.

The key point for Deleuze and Guattari is that it is theft or the seizure of what one has not produced (and does not need) that creates a point of surplus value of code. The despot becomes powerful, becomes socially valued and capable of organizing the socius, precisely through the seizure of excess. Prior, then, to an image of a world organized through exchange and governed by a maximization of utility, Deleuze and Guattari describe an intensively excessive desire, producing connections that are not relations of discrete terms. Rather, certain flows connect to produce a field (the 'body without organs' of the divine earth), and then this field or territory can be *de*territorialized when one point of flow (the despot) becomes a nexus of flows, creating a point that exceeds relations, resulting in a surplus value of code.[30] Excessive production is hoarded by the despot, and this produces him both as a privileged body and figures him as bearing a filiative relation to the earth. He becomes the king or chieftain with a divine right to rule because of his direct descent from the gods of the earth. By taking more (theft) a body does not just increase its own power but surpasses and enhances itself. Whereas coding produces connections of desire as relatively stable and regular, excessive consumption produces a surplus value of code – the despot is placed as bearing a divine relation to the system, just as capital is regarded as the meaning or reason of our systems.

If the first synthesis is productive, where desire is not desire *for* some already given being but produces a 'territory' in making its connection, the second synthesis is disjunctive: recording a series of terms across which desire passes – mouth or breast or penis or anus or earth. The third synthesis is *conjunctive*, and is effected from the surplus or excessive power of desire. If bodies produce *more* than is required for mere life then these excessive flows produce sites of power. (And one should think power here, not as *power over*, but as *power to*:[31] the organism that maintains mere survival does no more than that, but the organism that expends excess energy to create more also increases what it can do, but all this requires *speculation* or abandoning the maintenance of the present for what *might become*.) The child who recognizes itself as the object of the mother's desire and regards itself as the destination/conjunction of flows occurs only when the child is more than mere life and becomes the recipient of the mother's desire. This only occurs when it receives food as more than nourishment and as a gift or surplus. Then, the child appears as the centre or cause, rather than effect of relations. Here, Deleuze and Guattari reverse the oedipal logic whereby the child is first imagined as a self-present origin, fully at one with itself, and only then detached from the mother whom it feels to be lost, lacking, or prohibited. For Deleuze and Guattari there are relations – food to mouth, breast to lips, finger to cheek – that create certain regular flows from which the child can ulti- mately be recognized and then recognize itself as a point of conjunc- tion. Similarly, if from the flows of money and labour capitalism comes to appear as the law and logic of life *and* the site where surplus harnesses power (as in the accumulating capital of modern life, which no longer allows a moment of external excess) then the conjunction or effect of flows comes to appear as the system from which relations emerged. This is what happens in accounts of society as based on exchange. There can only be exchange once theft has produced some point that allows the flows to be coded. Exchange or relations among terms represses an intensive filiation. Ordinary points can emerge only because of singularities – potentials that organize or create a certain field of relations; such singular points always remain in excess of the system effected.

THE FICTION OF MIND

Deleuze's work prior to his collaboration with Guattari drew significantly upon psychoanalysis, both in his emphasis on the ways in which our orientation to sense is effected from bodily encounters (in *Logic of Sense*) and in various references in *Difference and Repetition* to a repetition that is not the repetition of some form or identity, but a perverse and 'deathly' repletion that destroys same- ness and unity, that abandons the self. Deleuze's references to Freud, and the highly psychoanalytic treatise of *Anti-Oedipus*, are all part of a larger philosophical project. Psychoanalysis does not accept that we begin as fully formed selves who then must know a world. Not only did Freud argue that the ego or thinking self was a mere part or image of a psychic system that comprised drives that never came to conscious reflection or presence, he was also insistent that the border between self and world was something that was effected

through time, and in relation to others. In this regard his work resonates with those philosophers who Deleuze regarded as having
opened up the question of univocity:[32] far from explaining the world
as the relation between two beings, such as mind and world, responsible and radical philosophy accounts for the emergence of this distinction between mind and world, knower and known, perceiver and
perceived. What is crucial in all this is the *image*: for Freud the ego
is the image the self has of itself as a unity, while for Deleuze the
history of philosophy has proceeded by working from an image of
thought, the image of the rational and organized self. What needs to
be understood is the creation or emergence of this image. How does
something like the brain come to understand itself as mind, and how
do human bodies come to imagine themselves as 'humanity'? The
image, for Deleuze, is not a surplus or fiction added on to some self-
present world-in-itself, for all thinking, perception, experience and
action – indeed, all life – *is a process of imaging or relations*. So how
is it that one image – the image of mind – came to be understood as
the origin of all images?[33]

In addition to his encounter with Freud and psychoanalysis
Deleuze's use of the history of philosophy drew upon authors who
explained the emergence of unities of sense from a synthesis or
process of life that was pre-personal. That is, rather than begin philosophy from the mind and then ask about the truth of the world,
and rather than assuming that the world possesses some stable logic
to be discovered, Deleuze focused on the philosophers who
explained the creation or genesis of the self and its perception of the
world. In his book on Leibniz, Deleuze explores the complexities of
the fold, where mind and matter are ways in which being is
unfolded.[34] We cannot begin from the separate substances of mind
and matter but must come to understand how mind is produced as
a series of perceptions and matter is unfolded as that which can be
perceived in a regular and lawful manner. In his book on Hume,
Deleuze describes the mind as a site where ideas are connected or
synthesized, such that fictions (including the self and the social
whole) are produced from within life.[35] In his book on Spinoza,
Deleuze reiterates a commitment to immanence in opposition to the
illusions of transcendence.[36] Mind is not a separate substance that
determines the world, nor is matter some separate and lifeless stuff
given form by mind; mind and matter are attributes of one dynamic
life, with these attributes being expressed in modes. So the human

being is one mode of thinking life, but humans can also be considered according to the attribute of matter, and this is perfectly legitimate when we consider the body. We need to see life both as thinking and as embodied, with neither attribute being less important or subordinated to the other. We can then realize the Spinozist philosophy of mind being 'an idea of the body', for what occurs as matter – certain physiological responses – can be lived at the level of mind; neither can be reduced to the other, for the life of the mind is of the same substance as life considered as matter. Biology considers the body as matter; philosophy considers the body as mind. The two attributes are different, and for this reason neither can be the cause or explanation of the other.

Deleuze's commitment to Spinoza's monism is one of the most important aspects of his philosophy, for it allows for a radical programme of demystification: there is no substance or life other than *this* one expressive life that we live. It is the task of philosophy to overcome the illusions of a God beyond this world. But we also need to understand how such illusions of transcendence emerge, and we can only do this if we consider how thought is immanent to a life that expresses itself in images. Deleuze's attention to the image in the history of philosophy is not a focus on the history of ideas. Deleuze draws upon a number of philosophers who refuse the idea of a subject or mind that imagines its world, and instead argue that mind is itself an image, and so we need to understand how life forms this image of a privileged viewer or subject. Some light is shed on this question in the work of Spinoza, for whom there are three levels of understanding. The highest level requires going beyond the world as it appears *for us*, beyond the world from our own interested and localized viewpoint to imagine the world as it is for all time. This would then mean not only overcoming the world as it is represented by 'man', but also overcoming the image of 'man' as the point from which the world is known.

In his book on Bergson, Deleuze describes the mind as a capacity to receive images; the mind is nothing other than this openness or receptivity but tends to mistake the image it forms of itself as a centre or origin of all imaging. As in his book on Hume, Deleuze emphasizes a fictive capacity of life. The idea of mind or 'man' as a centre of life occurs through the imagination; mind is first of all nothing other than a series of images which then creates an image of itself which it imagines to be somehow primary. And such a fiction or image of the human is, to a certain extent, life-enabling insofar as we form societies and collectives of those whom we also recognize in terms of this image; but life can only reach its fullest power by overcoming the image of the human as the centre of life and the world and intuiting worlds other than its own.[37] The Bergsonian method of intuition overcomes the anthropocentric illusion by striving for perceptions beyond the organizing image of 'man', recognizing that the image of the brain is one image among others. Bergson is, then, part of a Deleuzian history of philosophy where philosophy is not a discipline concerned with uncovering what mind *is*, so much as an interrogation into the production of images of thought and the quest for thought without an image. Deleuze's philosophical project, which has been dominated by the question of genesis – not accepting any being or image without asking how such an image comes into being – is therefore crucially tied to the question of synthesis, or the processes and connections from which recognizable forms emerge. His emphasis on the fictive power of the mind is, therefore, not so much an emphasis on mind's construction of its world as it is a project to examine the very creation and synthesis of the image of mind that has dominated Western thought.

Even Deleuze's seemingly less sympathetic book on Kant details the various synthetic processes – of reason, understanding and imagination – which create Ideas of totality, freedom and immortality. These Ideas are not, as Kant would have it, unified in a subject of good judgment, for they produce divergent and discordant demands.[38] According to Kant the Idea of freedom would enable us to be moral, while the Idea of a world with an original cause would help us to think a scientifically ordered world in accord with our own reason; and it would be aesthetic experience that would help us reflect on our mind's capacity to produce a world so conducive to moral and scientific judgment. For Deleuze, by contrast, the worlds of science, philosophy and art are incommensurable. The functions of science, the concepts of philosophy and the affects of art are not different aspects of one subject, but styles of thinking that open up planes. There is no pre-given harmony among these planes, so that the philosopher who encounters science or art has to give scientific or artistic thinking its new philosophical form. What Deleuze finds in Kant is the valuable distinction of the faculties. For Kant we should not see morality as something we can prove, nor should we see art as either morally good or rationally provable. But whereas

Kant insisted that there was a substrate that united these faculties – the transcendental subject who knows the limits of his reasoning and can distinguish between the beautiful, the good and the correct – Deleuze insists that we have to consider the ill will and malevolence of the subject, its capacity to create ill-formed, divergent and disharmonious connections.

In all cases, what Deleuze draws from the history of philosophy is an understanding of mind *not* as a reasoning centre that then confronts the world, but mind as an effect of images, images that are connected or synthesized to produce fictions. Such fictions have a power for they are not *added to* a real world; the world *is* a creative, desiring, perceiving life that exists only in its imaging relations.

COLLECTIVE INVESTMENT AND GROUP FANTASY

This emphasis on a synthesizing creative life that is real only insofar as it produces relations of imaging goes some way towards forming a political philosophy that is at odds with the notion of ideology. For according to Deleuze and Guattari, it is not as though there is a real world that is then more or less accurately perceived. Everything is perception, imaging, expression and synthesis; there is nothing that we can posit as being in itself prior to and beyond all relations. Not only could we never *know* something before all relations (for knowing itself is a relation); nothing could *be* non-relationally, for something to live or *be* it must go through time and have its place, and this requires even at the molecular level of life the establishing of relations and connections. So, while Deleuze refuses the idea of one set of relations – say, the human style of cognition – as definitive of the world, and while he also insists that different potentials might be actualized differently depending upon the relations they establish, he is nevertheless insistent that life does not exist in itself and then express itself through relations; life is just this production of connections and relations. To refer to this relationality as *perception* is to insist that each power or potential *to relate* opens up its own world. I might perceive the mosquito that is biting my arm, while the mosquito has some perception of my arm; but while my perception takes the form of a visual image and a sensation on my skin, the mosquito's perceptual orientation is towards the smell of acid and the surface of my arm. Beyond the world as I see it there are not only mosquito worlds but plant worlds and molecular worlds, different styles of relation or perception. The task of thinking is not to establish the truest or highest world but to think the multiplicity of perceptions that unfold divergent worlds.

> Desire stretches that far: desiring one's own annihilation, or desiring the power to annihilate. Money, army, police and State desire, fascist desire, even fascism is desire . . . It is a problem not of ideology but of pure matter, a phenomenon of physical, biological, psychic, social, or cosmic matter.[39]

This has direct political consequences when we think of the usual relation between desire and the image. We tend to think of individuals as having natural and appropriate desires that might then be distorted or deflected, either by themselves – where their less noble or base desires lead them astray – or by those in power – where women, the masses or the colonized are duped into a false understanding of their real interests. This notion of ideology as false consciousness or distortion of the real does have the political advantage of allowing a revolutionary group – Marxists or feminists – the right to point out what our real interests ought to be. But it also creates two problems: how is it that people come to desire what is only illusory, and by what right or power does the Marxist or feminist critic demystify those illusions?

Deleuze and Guattari refuse to place their work in a position of transcendence, outside desire and illusion, as though they and they alone could discern what we ought to desire. Instead they reject the ideological premise that desire is suffering from illusion or repression. On the contrary, they seek to explain how it is that fascism, racism and patriarchy *are desired*. It is not that we have been tricked into repressing our desires, and it is not as though there is some group – the capitalists – who create images that conceal the truth from us. Rather, we desire those very images that *are* fascism and patriarchy;[40] we invest positively in, indeed *we are*, the desire for the strong punishing father, the mother or femininity beyond the law, and the white reasoning face of 'man'.[41] What Deleuze and Guattari have to do is not point out that such images hide or conceal an underlying reality; for their politics of immanence insists upon the reality of images. Instead they have to show how such desiring images *work*: certain images turn power away from what it can do, while other images take power to its maximum. Take the case of woman, for example. It is not that there is a real femininity belied by stereotypes, for 'woman' is the historical result of a series of political relations whereby sexual difference is coded through the family or law. However, there is a *potentiality* from which the image of 'woman' was coded and which might be released from its governing image. The familial complex of mother–father–child though which the notion of 'woman' is defined, and where woman is the other of 'man', emerges from a much broader range of potentials; we can imagine bodies entering into different relations, with childbirth, sexual difference and sexual relations producing configurations that do not fit into the heterosexual dyad. If we were to think 'woman' not as something that is – such that we could dismiss certain predicates as 'unwomanly' – but as a potentiality from which the image of 'woman' has emerged, then we could arrive at 'becoming-woman'. For Deleuze and Guattari it is this concept which is the key to *all* becomings precisely because it is 'man' as the image of reason, thought, representation and action that has allowed the flow of life's images to be centred on a single governing image. If one image – 'man' – becomes the ground of all imaging then life's potentiality for connection, creation, mutation, deflection and becoming becomes limited by that image through which we perceive all other images. Their key methodological point is not to point to a better or more real image, for the familial image of mother–father–child is all too real and effective, but to insist that if life is a potential for imaging then that potential can only be maximized by not allowing any single image to govern all others. This is an ethics of life, defined not by what life is, but by the potential of life to open itself to what is not already given. Deleuze and Guattari do not celebrate the *negation* of life, or the power of life to *not* be itself or to be radically undetermined. Quite the reverse, for life has the power to create images of what is not yet given, to move or act according to the pathways it imagines: life is neither being nor non-being but '?being'.

For Deleuze and Guattari it is not the case that desires are deflected from their power by images that have *no reality* – images that are ideological because they *misrepresent*. Rather, desire turns against itself or is deflected from its own power *because it is creative*. It is here that Deleuze's book on Nietzsche is of crucial importance: all life is action and reaction, a creative force or becoming without a transcendent truth.[42] But certain creations – the idea of 'man' or a 'higher world' or even of the self as a centre of activity – serve to diminish life, turning creation against itself. In *Anti-Oedipus* this is referred to as anti-production. It is in this work with Guattari that the problem of reactive forces takes a form that Deleuze's more traditionally philosophical works would only intimate. How can desire's anti-production or reaction be explained without referring to some external, accidental or imposed cause? That is, how can we see capitalism and its denial of life not as an external corruption that befalls life but as one of life's potentialities? Further, how can we judge anti-production? If life does have a tendency not just to create, expand, produce and maximize, but also to destroy itself, how can we condemn certain forms of anti-production? Without appealing to a standard or norm beyond life, how do we judge certain forms or images as counter to life? If God, man, the good and humanity are effected fictions, how do we assess or criticize those fictions?

Anti-Oedipus is significant here because the development of the syntheses is no longer located in the mind as the site of perception but in groups. These are not groups of individuals, for the 'individual' is already a 'group fantasy' derived from collective investments. It is in this radical politicization of life that Deleuze and Guattari's work is at its most creative. Instead of beginning with individuals and then explaining the emergence of the polity, Deleuze and Guattari begin from groups of bodies that form the primitive socius and then ultimately explain the genesis of the private individual. Privacy is a group fantasy and has as its condition a history of molecular and micropolitical becomings.[43] Whereas psychoanalysis begins with the *human* condition – the infant who faces a mother whose desire it must address in order to live – Deleuze and Guattari explain how this Oedipal scene that supposedly explains politics is itself the effect of a political history. For psychoanalysis our entry into culture and our submission to law is the *result* of abandoning desire for our mothers, identifying with the authority of our fathers and then transferring that authority to the law as such, where law stands for the relations or structures that govern a life that would otherwise be undifferentiated, unmediated, lawless, inhuman and ahistorical. By contrast, Deleuze and Guattari argue that the very relation among bodies that produces the mother–child relation is itself political and cannot be used to explain politics. We do not, they argue, abandon desire for our mothers and therefore settle for a socially mediated desire; the image of the mother *as desired, as a lost object* is highly political and precisely what needs to be explained.

How, they ask, did we come to think of ourselves as submitted to a law that prohibits an impossible object? And how did we come to think of politics as ideology, as a system of signs that mediates a real world that can never be approached, thought or lived?

The history of capitalism, Deleuze and Guattari argue, is the history of *privatization*. That is, a paralogism or short-circuit of life's syntheses of images produces a false object or illusory cause; an effect – the image of 'man' – is taken for a cause, and then a whole series of disordered images ensues. Without appealing to a transcendent truth, or life as it really is outside the images we have of it, Deleuze and Guattari construct an immanent critique. Unlike ideology theory they do not see the illusion or paralogism as *imposed* upon life, but explain the emergence of images from a tendency of life that has not arrived at its fullest expression but has folded back upon itself, ceased to become and taken itself for a ground above and beyond life. If we look at the creative structure of life as an imaging power we will recognize the illegitimate use of 'man' as some organizing centre of images (as the supposed ground and cause of fantasy rather than one fantasy among others). We will then liberate desiring production from the private self and instead look at the production of privacy. This production is both historical, requiring a series of connections, and political, producing distinct social machines.

We can imagine the primitive socius of collective investments by thinking of a grouping of bodies that have no identity outside their perceptive relations – bodies assembled around the tribal phallus or animal totems. If the anus is privatized at this stage by becoming an object withdrawn from collective life and managed as devoid of sense, this is because the privatization of capitalism is a limiting tendency of life as such. That is, we do not have to wait for the appearance of money, where my labour and desire can now be traded and exchanged with any other and where the individual becomes an empty point where flows of money, goods and images intersect, for privatization to emerge. The creation of zones outside collective life – such as the anus – where there can be mere stuff (shit) that has no value or identity in itself is what makes modern capitalism possible. If we think of collective life as a multiplicity of perceptions, not yet organized from a single overarching point of view, then we can think of privatization as a tendency towards separation and abstraction; something detaches itself from the chaos and difference as an indifferent mere 'this'. If shit separates the anus from the collective, allowing for a hidden space outside the forces and negotiations of the polis, money is the extreme form of privatization, a vehicle that enables me to earn, live and manage my life while you earn, live and spend your own. Selves manage their own body and waste just as they will manage their desires through money and spending.

But it is also possible that such flows might be radically deterritorialized, and this is precisely what Deleuze and Guattari seek to do in *Anti-Oedipus*: to free desires, images and intensities from their location either in individuals or in specific systems of coding. Territories in the primitive socius are coded, marked explicitly in processes of tattooing, scarring, painting and piercing. Such processes allow organs such as the eyes, penis, breast or head to be experienced collectively. Indeed, it is not that I am an individual body that becomes one of a tribe by being marked; rather, there are organs that are marked, this marking produces an assemblage and territory of bodies, and it is only then possible that a body might – as it will do in modernity – take itself as an individual. But before the individual detaches or deterritorializes itself from the collective assemblage there occurs what Deleuze and Guattari refer to as the despotic socius. Whereas the bodies of a territory are coded through their markings as organs of that territory, it is possible that one body is decoded – removed from what is taken as this territory's life, desocialized, dehistoricized – and appears as a point outside those flows of life: in the case of the despot the marked bodies become overcoded by a body perceived as a site of power, as the origin of the flow. When the despot *enjoys* the collective rituals of scarring or tattooing a point of view is established outside the assemblage, a point of view that can then appear as the law or order of that assemblage.

Privatization, or the removal from explicitly collective life, is a potentiality of human life. In *Anti-Oedipus* Deleuze and Guattari describe the tendency which at once *codes* flows – semen, food, hunted animals and precious objects – *and* allows other flows *not* to enter into the production of the social machine: the flow of shit is waste, non-life or anti-production, a flow that must be mastered or overcome in order that we become social. At the basis of Deleuze and Guattari's focus on privatization is an argument regarding collective investment. In the beginning organs are invested collectively; the ritual of circumcision that is the object of the tribal gaze creates an assemblage of bodies *as* a tribe *at the same time* as the organ becomes charged with force. Only later, in modernity, will the phallus that was the focus of desiring bodies become the penis that the father of the Oedipus promise threatens to castrate.

At the heart of life there is collective investment or group fantasy; the body is directly and immediately political. The experience of the self in modernity as dominated by the head of reason, expressed through the eyes of the soul and the demeanour of the face, and sexualized through the private genital organs is the result of a specific political history. First, bodies need to be marked out as being of this specific group, then the group needs to be organized by an elevated or deterritorialized body – so that pain is now lived as the threatened punishment of the despot and pleasure is lived as a promised reward. Finally, this organizing moral body has to be internalized as one's own. This is what happens with the story of psychoanalysis, when 'we' all live the drama of Oedipus, castration, the surpassing of anal eroticism and so on. We might ask, for example, how something like 'the body' became thinkable: how did we come to organize ourselves into a mind that governs this physical substance; how was such a border or distribution effected? In order for the body, 'man' and ultimately all relations to become 'private' (as in capitalism) Deleuze and Guattari argue that a process of overcoding must have coupled itself to territorialization or the inscribing of investments.[44]

An investment, broadly speaking, is the regularity of a flow, a channelling of energy: the tendency for the mouth to couple with the breast, for bodies to dance around a particular image, for the heart-rate of a body to be elevated with the intrusion of a certain memory, for the eye to be drawn towards a ritual – all these connections do not just relate points, for the flow produces a charge or force that creates a relative stability in the chaotic flux of life. If any investment is governed by another flow, then there is overcoding. The bodies that dance or engage in a collective ritual of scarring may be viewed by a body that sets itself outside the field – deterritorialization – that then refers the relations among bodies to the threat of violence (the cruelty of overcoding).

THE TIME OF 'MAN'

Deleuze and Guattari follow Nietzsche in arguing for the production of memory through violence as *the* motor of human political history. In the cinema books, and in his work on Bergson, Deleuze creates a radical concept of time. In addition to the spatialized time of everyday life, or the time that is measured as a series of extended and equivalent units, there is also an intensive time, where each singular temporal flux reconfigures the open whole of life. Human memory and history is best understood in terms of the extended, inscribed and measurable time of Chronos. Human history, indeed humanity as such, is only possible through the carving out of memory. Nietzsche describes this process as 'festive cruelty': if a body can be marked, scarred, tortured or inscribed it becomes capable of living time in terms of a *debt*: 'I' become a continuous self if I can be held accountable for what I have been, *or* if I can be called upon to live up to a promise.[45] Even before there is an actual despot who threatens bodies, there is a primitive inscription such that a body's present pain is what opens any assemblage of bodies to a *line* of time. The scarring of bodies marks out a group that will be able to recognize, repeat and renew itself. Individual memory – holding experiences to be *mine* – depends upon collective memory; for there can only be 'mineness' or a concept of self if a stable body through time is constituted in such a way that later times can be reckoned according to an equivalent or comparable point of the past. The modern self who appears as the locus and cause of memory is actually the effect of a series of collective inscriptions. First, there is the marking out of groups of bodies as a territory, which is excessive or festive; the exertion of force occurs without this force being directed towards industry, work or saving time. Second, the marks are surveyed by an enjoying eye, which in extracting enjoyment can also promise further pain: if a scene of cruelty is commanded from above it becomes *terror*, and the time of the present force is referred back to its source in punishment and forwards to future possible threats. The body of 'man' becomes capable of bearing promises only when time is constituted in extension – a future answerable to the past, and a past held over by the anticipated future.

There is, therefore, a proto-capitalist quality to extended memory. The time of capital does not allow for life's excessive productions to produce anarchic or unanticipated relations; the energy of the present is committed in advance to a future that is a repetition of production in the same form. While capitalism brings the quantification and standardization of time to an explicit and dominating peak, the idea of a humanity that remains the same through time, lives according to a standard and regards the world as so much uniform space to be mastered, also relies on an extended time. Capitalist production, which measures time as labour and manages creation according to its capacity to produce desires that will elicit more money (or more spent time), is an extreme form of the process of coding and overcoding. Every point in time is like every other and can be measured, spent, rendered efficient or sold. We are no longer governed by external norms – whether they be religious, nationalist or tribal – for in liberalism all desires can be managed as aspects of 'my' life, where the subject or 'I' has *no* being other than a simple temporal continuity. 'I' have no being outside my actions, memories or desires, and my body is nothing more than the locus of this self-synthesizing transcendental subject. Deleuze and Guattari's political and social theory refuses any constituted form in order to examine the flows that make identities, forms and relatively stable points possible.

THE INTENSE GERMINAL INFLUX

One way of understanding continental philosophy is to consider the tradition that runs from Kant to Deleuze as post-metaphysical. In his *Critique of Pure Reason* Kant was both critical of metaphysics – for he insisted that philosophers were caught up in unanswerable questions, such as the problems of God, free will and immortality of the soul – at the same time as he thought we should ask how and why such metaphysical questions emerged. What is thinking such that it can pose itself insoluble problems, problems beyond its own domain? Kant argued that we have knowledge through experience, and so it is illegitimate to make pronouncements about what lies beyond experience – the metaphysical and the supersensible. He made a distinction between theory and practice, or what we can know and what we can do; and he also made a distinction within theory between what we can know about the world through experience, and *pure* reason or the mind's forms that we apply to the world. We cannot have theoretical knowledge of God, the infinite or the soul in the same way that we can of scientific phenomena that are limited by experience. We can *think* of such Ideas – this is pure reason – and we can act *as if* there were a God, freedom and immortality – this is practical; but we cannot pass from some experience of God to know what we ought to do. There is a gap, therefore, between pure reason and practical reason, what we can know and what we ought to do. For the post-Kantian tradition this gap was bridged by the aesthetic. In an experience of beauty we *feel* the order and form of what is given, *as though* what we experienced were perfectly formed for the understanding's power to bring it to concepts. In the sublime we *feel* the inability of the mind to make sense of what is given.[46] In both cases this feeling of the mind's forming power indicates the supersensible – that we are forming powers not reducible to the world's experienced form.[47] This would then reinforce the *Idea* that we can act as if we were free, as if we could be moral, or not determined by worldly self-interest.

What Kant's post-metaphysical philosophy raised was a problem that maintained itself in contemporary poststructuralism and that motivated many of Deleuze's critical endeavours: this is the transcendental problem, the problem of beginning philosophy or thinking. How can we really question what we do and think if we are already operating with assumed images? It is not sufficient, though, to pass from this question of the form or sense we make of the world to a *simple* constructivism, or the idea that all truth is merely the creation of the mind. For this leaves two questions. For Deleuze we need to ask how this image of mind or subject is formed – how is it that one image came to appear as the image from which chaos is organized? Second, how do we explain pure truth or the power to reason in general, regardless of this or that specific experience? It is this problem that sets Deleuze apart from any simple postmodern relativism, for he does *not* argue that thought or the subject can make of the world what it will; he is critical both of the idea of *the* subject and of the rejection of science as one more fiction. Indeed, one of the dominant concerns of his work is science's capacity to give a consistency to chaos, with these forms being irreducible to the subject, mind or experience. For Kant, however, the sciences did yield pure formal truths, and these pure forms or categories are transcendental to experience; they make experience possible. For Deleuze a truly transcendental philosophy does not rely on the categories or forms that the subject brings to experience, but explains the emergence of those forms or categories.

Poststructuralism in both its Deleuzean and Derridean forms does not reject all notions of truth; on the contrary, it extends Kant's problem of the inhumanity or purely formal nature of truth. For Kant, for example, geometry is possible not because the truths of space are beyond experience but because there are certain forms – such as the spatial distinction between inner and outer, here and there – without which *no* experience would be possible. The ideal truths of geometry apply to our actual world precisely because the world we live is always already lived through the sense we make of it. We can only know the truths of geometry after having laid them out in experience, but they also extend beyond any particular experience to experience in general. For Kant this yielded the truth both of pure reason, which is the power of the subject to synthesize or connect series *beyond* actual experience, and the truth of the understanding, which are the truths of reason in relation to experience. We can have a rigorous theory of space, such as geometry, because on the one hand we have reason as a synthesizing and ordering capacity and, on the other hand, we have intuition or the given that we synthesize. *Pure* reason takes the synthesizing power and extends it beyond what might be intuited. So, whereas it is legitimate to experience the world as a causal sequence because without the ordering of causes and effects we would not even have coherent experience, it is illegitimate to extend that series beyond experience. For something to be experienced by a subject it has to be other than that subject, and therefore located in a conditioned series of temporal and spatial points. If we try to think of some first cause, something that begins the series of conditions, then we commit an error or an illegitimate use of the synthesis. We take a form that makes experience possible, such as temporal order, and try to think the beginning or being of that order. Kant argues that this pure use of reason – thinking the series itself without it being the series *of* any experienced manifold – is illegitimate theoretically. However, it does have *practical* import. For it is our capacity to think beyond causality that allows us to form the Idea (but not the knowable object) of freedom. If we can think of a free being, one who would act without any determining cause other than its own will to act, we can imagine what it would be to act for the sake of law.

In contemporary moral theory much is still made of this ability to imagine oneself as an end in itself, and not part of a causal sequence.[48] Liberalism, for example, is a general political principle that accepts that it is precisely because we are *not* given any determined law for how to act that we can only imagine ourselves as self-legislating, and cannot therefore act in ways that would impede others' capacity for self-legislation.[49] The law would be purely formal, not dictating this or that way in which we must live but precluding us from determining how any other in particular must live. The only law, then, is a law that would apply to any possible will; one could neither make an exception for oneself or for others by giving particular preferences legal or moral weight. Law, for Kant, is the Idea of what one would do regardless of particular circumstances, so the moral law is just that Idea of how one might act in the absence of being caused. This gives us the *Idea* of morality, and while we may never in fact arrive at this position of a pure free will we can nevertheless – practically – act as though such freedom were possible. This would give us the Idea of humanity that did not act for itself as a pathological being (governed by feelings and desires) but only by *pure action*, an act that would be done by any agent whatever, regardless of one's position within experience. It is because we cannot know what lies beyond experience for Kant that our thought of this 'beyond' gives us an idea of freedom; our *not* knowing any determined form of the law gives us the responsibility for determining the law for ourselves. There cannot, then, be any transition from what we know about this or that human being or body – *what is*, or what we know – to what we ought to do. However, there is a direct transition from what we can imagine beyond the knowable – I can imagine myself as a free uncaused will – to what we ought to do: I *can* implies I *ought*.

Now, on the one hand, Deleuze is insistent that Kant has not gone far enough in breaking away from a determined image of 'man' or humanity. Kant claims to be thinking of a pure will, free from all interested and determined images; he claims to be thinking transcendentally. But, according to Deleuze, the transcendental subject that synthesizes the world is not truly transcendental; for it relies on moving from one image – the image of a reason that strives to master the world and reduce different experiences to formerly established models – and then sees that image as the origin of all images. However, despite Kant's reliance on common sense and good sense, or the idea that 'the subject' can be assumed to be naturally oriented towards consensus and harmony, Kant's theory of the three faculties also allows for a theory of discordance and the Idea. For Kant, the understanding is the faculty that orders intuited data into concepts; so this manifold of colour I see before me can be subsumed under the concept of 'tree'. Reason is the faculty that gives form to our ordered experience, locating all events in some causal chain – as experience could not be possible if there were not some notion that this was the experience *of* some world, and the very notion of an objective world requires some causality (even if we can imagine quite different causal connections from our own world). The imagination is what allows for received impressions to be placed in some minimal form so that they might be given concepts, so that we have to see the manifold in some sort of style before conceptualizing it as a tree. Kant had argued that beauty occurs with the harmony of imagination and understanding: if a landscape I am viewing is of such a symmetrical, bounded and evenly distributed proportion that I do not have to make an intellectual effort to identify it, then before I have even conceptualized it *as* this or that natural phenomenon I can *feel* the easy relation between understanding and imagination. It is this feeling which I can reflect upon and recognize as beauty, so that beauty is neither arbitrary – just what I in particular feel – nor theoretically provable, as there can be no pre-given rules to produce this feeling. It is singular and universal. However, this feeling of harmony does give us a sense of how all humanity *would feel*, and also gives us a feeling of how nature seems to be in accord with our experience of it. The other accord of the faculties Kant discusses is the sublime. Here the imagination is *unable* to give a bounded form to its experience, so that there cannot be a simple act of the understanding's recognition; but in striving to go beyond what can be intuited in a finite and bound style the subject experiences a feeling of the infinite and unbounded, or that which lies beyond representation. Reflecting on this experience of the boundless 'we' can feel that we are not subjects bound by the material finite world. In both cases aesthetic or reflective experience allows us to feel, but not know, our status as subjects not determined by the physical world of objects bounded in causal time and space.

It is this aspect of Kant's doctrine of the faculties that Deleuze both expands and corrects. Like Kant, Deleuze often expresses the positivity of the Idea:[50] we may not be able to present the infinite as some image within our experience of time and space, but we can *think* of extending the series of causality beyond any experienced series, and we can think of extending the syntheses of space beyond any bounded object.

Whereas Kant will argue that this ultimately gives us a feeling of the 'supersensible substrate of humanity' which 'we' all are, thus producing an ultimate harmony or 'sensus communis', Deleuze will argue that the extension of syntheses beyond finite and bounded forms unhinges the subject, producing discordance and a shock to thought. Far from giving us the feeling of an underlying harmony or reasoning subject, the syntheses can be liberated from an 'image of thought' and extended beyond the human point of view. This will yield a social and political understanding of both the syntheses and the Idea. The syntheses will become forms of combination which produce the image of 'man'; man is not the founder of the syntheses. In *Anti-Oedipus* and *A Thousand Plateaus* Deleuze and Guattari look at the ways in which bodies are the results of genetic syntheses over time – the connections of certain evolutionary potentials until organisms are formed as relatively stable – and then they look at the ways in which human bodies as parts of the 'intense germinal influx' become connected in territories until, in modernity, something like the 'subject' appears to be the origin of synthesis, when it is actually an effect of historical, political and contingent connections. Their task, then, is not necessarily to destroy the modern subject so much as discern its production from flows of desire. One way of achieving this task is to return to the Kantian concept of the Idea but then to extend that Idea beyond the subject. Kant had argued that we cannot intuit or know freedom, because we can only know events *within* time and causation. Freedom as uncaused and a pure beginning could not be located within a represented time. However, even though we can have no experience or knowledge of freedom, we can have an Idea of freedom. We form this Idea by extending our rational capacity, which allows us to experience the world in a causal order, and then *think* of that which is uncaused or that which inaugurates a series. Ideas are formed by extending the conditions of experience beyond experience. They are not actual things, which we might know and study, so they could not be theoretical, but they would have practical import. If we can *think* of ourselves as free then we act differently: I can imagine that I am not a determined, interested automaton but one who is capable of imagining myself as an end, not a means. In such a case I would act morally, and it is this image of myself as a free and undetermined end, as a member of 'humanity', that yields an elevating feeling of respect. For Deleuze and Guattari, though, the Idea is *not* human; indeed it allows us to think beyond human life, and it is perhaps this aspect of Deleuze and Guattari's politics and Deleuze's philosophy that distances their work from any form of vitalism.

Henri Bergson, in *Creative Evolution*, argues that the intellect is originally formed in order to master life, so that the human mind sees the world only in terms that interest it, and cannot perceive the fluxes and durations of a life beyond its own; the world is perceived as so much inert matter. However, as the intellect becomes increasingly complex it can take two paths. First, mind can start to imagine itself as yet one more stable physical thing, and this is indeed what happens with crude forms of social determinism, psychology, sexism, racism or nationalism when we imagine minds or perceivers to be things with determined and unchanging qualities. This is what happens when 'man' becomes a norm or model which reifies all experience into a stable and unchanging form. Or, mind can take its cue, not from the physical sciences but from *life*, and understand that it is itself part of a flux of change, movement and creations. Mind is no longer the fixed point that watches a world pass by; it intuits itself as part of an open and living whole that is never given as an object and that harbours no point from which it could be fixed, determined or definitively ordered. The real world is one of processes rather than things, and mind is one more living process among others. The implication in Bergson's work, however, is that *humanity* will be the privileged duration that will be capable of overcoming its own located point of observation (its own folding of the world around itself) and will come to view the durations of other living flows. For Deleuze and Deleuze and Guattari, however, there is a further emphasis on an overcoming of humanity. Humanity will recognize itself, not as the subject set over against a world to be viewed but as a flow of duration among other durations, and it will also recognize that the coming into appearance of other durations – the image of time in its pure state – is given not through the mind's power of intuition but though machines: both contingent material machines, such as the camera that creates syntheses of images impossible for the bodily eye, and social machines that allow for practices such as philosophy, art and science that create concepts, affects and functions allowing for images that do not emerge or unfold from organic life.

CONCLUSION

Despite the fact that poststructuralism was always opposed to the idea that 'we' construct the world though language, or that 'we' are effects of language, the *reading* of poststructuralism in the English-speaking world has been language dominated. This is why, perhaps, it was given such a derisory reading by thinkers such as Jürgen Habermas, who described the tradition of French thought as a direct consequence of the collapse of the relation between philosophy and literature, a loss of the sense that there could be anything like a critical reason. There have been strong defences of Derrida against claims of linguistic determinism and relativism,[1] but Deleuze neither brought such charges nor gained the widespread appeal that was won by Derrida, Foucualt, Lyotard and Baudrillard. Part of the reason for the delay of interest in Deleuze[2] lay in his different attitude to language. At a time when political, film, literary and feminist theory were dominated by 'discourse', 'representation' and 'signification', Deleuze's and Deleuze and Guattari's emphasis on life was incommensurable with the dominant style of criticism. Today, however, the turn to Deleuze has both created and been enabled by a sense of the death of the linguistic paradigm. This in turn has led to an emphasis on 'life' and the sciences of life in literary, social, political and film theory. What I have tried to argue in this book is that Deleuze is a valuable thinker for just this reason: not only does he refuse to regard discourse, signification, representation or systems as adequate starting points for theory, he also explains *why* thinking is seduced into the illusion of transcendence. Rather than question just how images emerge from life we explain life from some already formed image. But if it is now recognized that we cannot explain life by reference to some system, such as discourse, language or the subject, there is nevertheless a tendency to begin the explanation of how systems emerge from life by beginning with a privileged image of the life of the organism. This is where the real challenge of Deleuze's philosophy lies, and it is for this reason that I would like to conclude with two quotations. The first is from *Anti-Oedipus* and was quoted in the Introduction to this book:

> The body without organs is the model of death . . . The death model appears when the body without organs repels the organs and lays them aside: no mouth, no tongue, no teeth – to the point of self-mutilation, to the point of suicide. Yet there is no real opposition between the body without organs and the organs as partial objects; the only real opposition is to the molar organism that is their common enemy . . . Hence it is absurd to speak of a death desire that would presumably be in qualitative opposition to the life desires. Death is not desired, there is only death that desires, by virtue of the body without organs or the immobile motor, and there is also life that desires, by virtue of the working organs.[3]

This is what sets Deleuze apart from the current trend in philosophy to think of life in terms of the life of the organism. Nothing is more evident, according to recent work in both philosophy and neuroscience, that life strives to maintain itself. According to Andy Clark, we should do away with the idea of mind as some kind of centralized 'manager' and see mind as extended, embodied, active and oriented to survival; we are not thinkers who *then* make our way in the world but organisms who have all sorts of capacities to extend and develop in response to our environments.[4] The commitment to self-maintaining life is given explicit scientific articulation in the work of Antonio Damasio:

> . . . the urge to stay alive is not a modern development. It is not a property of humans alone. In some fashion or other, from simple to complex, most living organisms exhibit it. What does vary is the degree to which organisms *know* about that urge. Few do. But the urge is still there whether organisms know of it or not. Thanks to consciousness, humans are keenly aware of it. Life is carried out inside a boundary that defines a body . . .
> . . . minds and consciousness, when they eventually appeared in evolution, were first and foremost about life and the life urge within a boundary. To a great extent they still are.[5]

Deleuze does, of course, both anticipate and endorse many of the arguments for embodied, purposive and striving life that now dominate philosophy, science and even explanations of art.[6] But if that were all Deleuze were doing we could now throw away our Deleuze (and all our art, literature and film) and go back to the nuts and bolts of biological and physical life. However, the reason why Deleuze does *not* begin or end his explanations from the image of the self-maintenance of the organism is precisely why he is worth reading. This reason is expressed clearly in the cinema books: the human sensory-motor apparatus has been dominated by self-maintenance and action according to self-maintenance. However, the human perceptive apparatus *also* has a potential to break with action and self-organization: to see as such, without that point of view being folded around *my* organizing striving centre. It is precisely the image of *bounded* life that Deleuze sees as *the* illusion that has dominated philosophy and that is overcome in the radical connections of art. This gives us two conclusive and concluding challenges. First, of course, we can explain art's emergence from life. V. S. Ramachandran, for example, has argued that we enjoy a Picasso because it activates the neurological facial recognition capacitites that have been so useful for our survival. But Deleuze's philosophy focuses on the way all potentials diverge from their emergence. In his book on Francis Bacon, for example, Deleuze describes the way the painter works *against* the tendencies towards recognition, towards the pleasure and stability of the human apparatus. This project of destroying human equilibrium was explicit in the surrealist movement, which directed itself directly against the tendencies of the brain to create habitual connections. But Deleuze also argued in his book on Leibniz and the baroque that the tendency for the human body to fold its perceptions around its own point of view was undone by an art that tried to create multiple foldings; the baroque art of folds gave a figure to the potentialities of matter's own movements, and also tried to express the unfolding of an image of the mind as interior.[7] This art did not begin with the image of the embodied mind but used matter to reflect on the relation between inner and outer, mind and matter, folding and unfolding. Art, then, has a reflective virtual power; it does not only emerge from tendencies towards self-maintenance but can also takes those tendencies as its object, working to destroy the images of harmony, homeostasis and equilibrium.

The second challenge follows from this and is more difficult. How do we justify such a philosophy that would seek to destroy images of life for the sake of life? Consider the opposite project, the project of a simple vitalism: all life is self-maintaining and all life strives for its own continuity. If this were so then anything that is living is good; anything that is destructive is bad. We move directly from life to ethics. But, as contemporary ethics and politics demonstrate, no such direct transition is possible, for it is always a question of *whose* life. Not only are political divisions between supposed pro-life and pro-choice campaigns incapable of being decided on the basis of life (for one supports the life of the foetus, the other the life of the mother); it is also the case that political and ethical thinking is closed down by appeals to life. If we can do philosophy and criticism without an image of life – if we can free thought from its home in the human sensory-motor apparatus – then we might start to think the difficult and ethical questions.[8] Not: is this or is this not life? But: what style[9] of life? How much difference from organized harmonious life – how much thinking – can we bear?

'Even when they are nonliving, or rather inorganic, things have a lived experience because they are perceptions and affections.'[10] This quotation from *What is Philosophy?* offers us the possibility of new problems and new styles of thinking. What is it to say that *even the nonliving* has the potential for perception? It may be the case, for example, that a living being – 'man' – creates a machine to further his life; such a machine might be a camera, a language or a bodily practice such as a ritualistic dance that binds a community together. But if even the nonliving can function or live then we have to entertain the possibility that such machines might go on to create connections that now have no basis in the *living* body from which they emerged. The practices of cinema might create connections and images destructive of the coherence of humanity. The language machine might create distortions that preclude communication. As an example we can think of all the copying errors, lacunae or possible accidental marks that pervade the canon of literature. The movements of the body the constitute tribal dance and that serve a territorializing function of producing an assemblage of bodies can also be repeated, circulated, distorted and quoted so that they now move and differ for themselves – *de*territorialized from their functional and 'human' home. The challenge of Deleuze's philosophy is therefore twofold: on the one hand, there is the project of genesis, or not accepting the existence of a system or assemblage but asking how that system emerges from life. On the other hand, and this is where art and philosophy become important, we can also see how life creates series of difference that are discontinuous or fractured from their originating impulse: 'not all Life is confined to the organic strata: rather, the organism is that which life sets against itself in order to limit itself, and there is a life all the more intense, all the more powerful for being anorganic.'[11]

NOTES

INTRODUCTION

1 Alain Badiou, *Deleuze: The Clamor of Being*, trans. Louise Burchill, Minneapolis: University of Minnesota Press, 2000.
2 AO 329.
3 AO 330.
4 B 98.
5 That Deleuze is a philosopher of the *future*, and not a philosopher who would trace expression back to its origins, was noted early by Elizabeth Grosz and is explored fully in her recent work, *In the Nick of Time*, Sydney: Allen and Unwin, 2004.
6 DR xvi.
7 DR xx.
8 WP 154.
9 LB 130.
10 LS 76.
11 I use the term inhuman here, not in the sense of *lacking* some quality of humanity, but in Deleuze's positive sense that there is a world of life, affect and synthesis well beyond the domain of 'man'.
12 In addition to Alain Badiou's criticism of Deleuze as a neo-Platonist, there has also been a vibrant clarification of Deleuze's philosophy as a resource for analytical philosophy grounded in solid scientific principles. See Manuel DeLanda, *Intensive Science and Virtual Philosophy*, London: Continuum, 2002.
13 It is therefore important to consider the ways in which Deleuze's work has been created anew – and not simply 'applied' – in further encounters with literature, film and politics. Examples of creative elaborations of Deleuze's work abound but for an overview see Ronald Bogue, *Deleuze on Cinema*, London: Routledge, 2003; Ronald Bogue, *Deleuze on Literature*, London: Routledge, 2003, and Ronald Bogue, *Deleuze on Music, Painting and the Arts*, London: Routledge, 2003. For a detailed argument for the extension rather than clarfication of Deleuze's philosophy, see Ian Buchanan, *Deleuzism: A Metacommentary*, Edinburgh: Edinburgh University Press, 2000.

1: CINEMA, THOUGHT AND TIME

1 For an exploration of this quotation from Deleuze see Gregory Flaxman (ed.), *The Brain is a Screen: Deleuze and the Philosophy of Cinema*, Minneapolis: University of Minnesota Press, 2000.

2 For one of the most speculative projects extending the Deleuzian legacy see Rosi Braidotti, *Metamorphoses: Towards a Materialist Theory of Becoming*, Cambridge: Polity, 2002.

3 On the philosophical background to this problem, see Martin Heidegger, *The Question Concerning Technology, and Other Essays*, William Lovitt (trans.), New York: Harper and Row, 1977, but for a Greek etymological definition, see J. O. Urmson, *The Greek Philosophical Vocabulary*, London: Duckworth, 1990.

4 Recent work in neuroscience confirms the claims made by both Bergson and Deleuze that the human eye–brain composes and synthesizes its data, 'seeing' a full and stable picture from what is actually or physically unstable, discontinuous and partial, but also selecting from 'superabundance'. See L. Pessoa, E. Thomson and A. Noe, 'Finding Out about Filling In: A Guide to Perceptual Completion for Visual Science and the Philosophy of Perception', *Behavioural and Brain Sciences,* 21 (1998), 723–48.

5 Andy Clark, *Natural Born Cyborgs: Minds, Technologies, and the Future of Human Intelligence*, Oxford: Oxford University Press, 2003.

6 Henri Bergson, *Creative Evolution*, trans. Arthur Mitchell, New York: Henry Holt, 1911, p. 306.

7 C1 208–9.

8 Jacques Derrida, *Margins of Philosophy*, trans. Alan Bass, Chicago: University of Chicago Press, 1982.

9 Luce Irigaray, *Speculum of the Other Woman*, trans. Gillian C. Gill, Ithaca, NY: Cornell University Press, 1985.

10 PS 41; TP 407–8.

11 Jacques Derrida, *Raising the Tone of Philosophy: Late Essays by Immanuel Kant, Transformative Critique by Jacques Derrida*, ed. Peter Fenves, Baltimore, MA: Johns Hopkins University Press, 1993.

12 TP 277.

13 Henri Bergson, *The Two Sources of Morality and Religion*, trans. R. Ashley Audra and C. Brereton, Indiana: University of Notre Dame Press, 1963.

14 TP 329.

15 TP 176.

16 For a philosophical reading of Deleuze's relation to Bergson that emphasizes the relation to life while also insisting that 'life' is not reducible to biological or physical life, see Keith Ansell Pearson, *Germinal Life: The Difference and Repetition of Deleuze*, London: Routledge, 1999.

17 DR 276.

18 Edmund Husserl also founded the project of phenomenology on a commitment to immanent life; practices such as geometry and mathematics ought not to be simply accepted as true but need to be demonstrated as having their genesis in one flowing temporally self-constituting conscious

life. Edmund Husserl, *The Crisis of European Sciences and Transcendental Phenomenology: An Introduction to Phenomenological Philosophy*, trans. David Carr, Evanston: Northwestern University Press, 1970. Prior to Husserl, the late nineteenth century witnessed an efflorescence of radically historicist thinking: 'man' does not go through time, for there is no unchanging subject that subtends the ongoing difference of historical change. Rather, time and history become transcendental horizons from which 'man' emerges as a being that can turn back and discern his own unfolding. See Michel Foucault, *The Order of Things*, London: Tavistock, 1970.

19 Henri Bergson, *Creative Evolution*, p. 265.
20 Keith Ansell Pearson, *Philosophy and the Adventure of the Virtual: Bergson and the Time of Life*, London: Routledge, 2002, p. 12.
21 TP 33.
22 Manuel de Landa, *Intensive Science and Virtual Philosophy*, London: Continuum, 2002.
23 DR 177.
24 TP 485–6.
25 See Stephen Kern, *The Culture of Time and Space: 1880–1918*, Cambridge, MA: Harvard University Press, 1983.
26 David Bennett, 'Burghers, Burglars and Masturbators: The Sovereign Spender in the Age of Consumerism', *New Literary History*, 30: 2 (Spring 1999), 269–94.
27 David Rodowick, *Gilles Deleuze's Time Machine*, Durham, NC: Duke University Press, 1997.
28 DR 88.
29 PS 45.
30 WP 23.
31 B 2. Henri Bergson, *The Creative Mind*, trans. M. L. Andison, Totowa, NJ: Littlefield; Adams and Company, 1965, p. 11. On Deleuze's relation to Bergson and the method of intuition, see Keith Ansell Pearson, *Germinal Life: The Difference and Repetition of Deleuze*, London: Routledge, 1999.
32 LS 109.
33 K 41.
34 K 19.
35 Henri Bergson, *The Two Sources of Morality and Religion*.
36 Henri Bergson, *Duration and Simultaneity*, trans. L. Jacobson, Indianapolis: Bobbs-Merrill, 1956.
37 TP 4.

2: THE MOVEMENT-IMAGE

1 Cl 4.
2 Martin Heidegger, *What is a Thing?*, trans. W. B. Barton and Vera Deutsch, Lanham: University Press of America, 1985.
3 Immanuel Kant's transcendental argument for space and time as pure forms of intuition is the clearest and most influential example of this

argument, first articulated by Kant in his *Critique of Pure Reason* in 1781. Edmund Husserl's *On the Phenomenology of the Consciousness of Internal Time* (1893–1917) maintains the idea of the transcendental subject whose syntheses allow for the flow of one foundational time.

4 TP 299, 312.
5 TP 65.
6 DR 56.
7 DR 57.
8 Slavoj Žižek (ed.), *Everything You Wanted to Know About Lacan: (But were Afraid to Ask Hitchcock)*, London: Verso, 1992.
9 Joan Copjec, *Read My Desire: Lacan Against the Historicists*, Cambridge, MA: MIT Press, 1994.
10 This is why, for example, Judith Butler insists upon the necessity of *subjection* (Judith Butler, *The Psychic Life of Power: Theories in Subjection*, Stanford, CA: Stanford University Press, 1997).
11 C2 262.
12 AO 327.
13 Jacques Lacan, *Écrits*, trans. Alan Sheridan, London: Norton, 1977.
14 C1 6.
15 LS 104–5.
16 C1 11.
17 DR 245.
18 C1 40.
19 B 104–5.
20 C1 17.
21 K 221–2.
22 CC 5.
23 C1 46.
24 C1 48.
25 For such an uncharitable dismissal of postmodernism and its supposed over-dependence on a 'literary' view of the world, see Jürgen Habermas's *Philosophical Discourse of Modernity: Twelve Lectures Habermas*, trans. Frederick Lawrence, Cambridge: Polity, 1987.
26 WP 154.
27 C1 58.
28 C1 64.
29 C1 64–5.
30 C1 66.
31 B 27.
32 Brian Massumi, 'The Autonomy of Affect', in *Observing Complexity: Systems Theory and Postmodernism*, ed. William Rasch and Cary Wolfe, Minneapolis: University of Minnesota Press, pp. 273–97.
33 C1 66.
34 C1 80–1.
35 C1 146.
36 C1 118.
37 C1 111.
38 C1 98.

39 C1 99.
40 C1 102.
41 C1 99.
42 C1 100.
43 C1 197.
44 TP 114.
45 C2 34.
46 TP 313.
47 C1 198.
48 C1 200.
49 C1 203.
50 Niall Lucy, *Postmodern Literary Theory*, Oxford: Blackwell, 1997.
51 C1 215.
52 C1 31.
53 C2 31.
54 C2 32–3.
55 C2 33.

3: ART AND TIME

1 Bergson refers to the example of swimming in *Creative Evolution*, and this is then taken up by Deleuze in *Difference and Repetition*, 192.
2 Nietzsche, Friedrich, *Untimely Meditations*, trans. R. J. Hollingdale, Cambridge, UK: Cambridge University Press, 1997.
3 C2 80.
4 C2 88.
5 C2 80.
6 C2 76–7.
7 LS 161.
8 C2 77.
9 John Carey, *The Intellectuals and the Masses: Pride and Prejudice among the Literary Intelligentsia, 1880–1939*, London: Faber, 1992. Pierre Bourdieu, *Distinction: A Social Critique of the Judgement of Taste*, trans. Richard Nice. London: Routledge & Kegan Paul, 1984.
10 Germaine Greer, *The Female Eunuch*, London: MacGibbon & Kee, 1970.
11 WP 99, italics in the original.
12 C2 78.
13 C2 78, italics in the original.
14 C2 78.
15 C2 81.

4: ART AND HISTORY

1 LS 318.
2 On Deleuze's concepts and their relation to Derrida, see Paul Patton, *Deleuze and the Political*, London: Routledge, 2000.

3 WP 168.
4 WP 193.
5 WP 196.
6 They are therefore closer to Virginia Woolf's and D. H. Lawrence's modernisms than the history and tradtion of Joyce, Pound and Eliot. Lawrence and Woolf both theorized an art that stepped outside of human life in its historical constitution so that life as such could be given form in art. Eliot, Pound and Joyce, by contrast, used the Western tradition, canon or history of voices to broaden the modern and urban contraction of experience into functional and efficient 'man'.
7 Jane Goldman, *Modernism*, London: Palgrave, 2003.
8 WP 202.
9 WP 172.
10 Martin Heidegger, *Poetry*, *Language*, *Thought*, New York: Harper Colophon, 1971.
11 WP 172.
12 WP 174.
13 DR 245.
14 See the Blake archive at: www.blakearchive.org.
15 TP 41.
16 For an analysis of the specifics of Blake's technique, see Robert N. Essick, *William Blake*, *Printmaker*, Princeton, NJ : Princeton University Press, 1980.
17 WP 175.
18 WP 212.
19 WP 212.
20 WP 213.
21 WP 212.
22 WP 197.
23 WP 167.
24 Stuart Sim, *Beyond Aesthetics: Confrontations with Poststructuralism and Postmodernism*, Toronto: University of Toronto Press, 1992.
25 Fredric Jameson, *Postmodernism, or the Cultural Logic of Late Capitalism*, London: Verso, 1991.
26 David Bennett, 'Parody, Postmodernism and the Politics of Reading', *Critical Quarterly*, 27:4 (Winter 1985), 27–43.
27 Linda Hutcheon, *A Poetics of Postmodernism: History, Theory, Fiction*, Routledge: London, 1988.
28 Ihab Hassan, *The Postmodern Turn: Essays in Postmodern Theory and Culture*, Columbus: Ohio State University Press, 1987.
29 FB 86.
30 PS 49.
31 TP 12.
32 TP 174–5; 306–7.
33 WP 197.
34 Gary Genosko, *Félix Guattar: An Aberrant Introduction*, London: Continuum, 2002.
35 WP 193.

36 WP 193.
37 John Protevi has made much of this point as it is articulated in
   A Thousand Plateaus, where Deleuze and Guattari distinguish between
   the architect, who operates with a predetermined form, technique or
   structure, and the artisan, who follows the potentialities of matter.
   Protevi stresses the political significance of this distinction, which has
   revolutionary force in a Western culture that has privileged the 'hylo-
   morphic' model, or the imposition of form on undifferentiated, formless
   or chaotic matter. John Protevi, *Political Physics: Deleuze, Derrida, and
   the Body Politic*, New Brunswick, NJ: Athlone Press, 2001.
38 WP 193.
39 WP 192.
40 WP 193.
41 WP 193.
42 WP 193.
43 WP 194.
44 WP 195.
45 PS 111.
46 WP 196.
47 WP 195.

5: POLITICS AND THE ORIGIN OF MEANING

1 For an outline of Edmund Husserl's phenomenology, and definitions
   of the noeisis and noema, see Dermot Moran, *Introduction to
   Phenomenology*, London: Routledge, 2000.
2 LS 200.
3 Deleuze also referred to the virtual object in *Difference and Repetition*
   (p. 99).
4 In his book on Deleuze, *Organs Without Bodies*, Slavoj Žižek argues that
   there are two Deleuzes: the Deleuze who, in *The Logic of Sense*, recognized the truth of the Lacanian theory of the incorporeal and sterile
   nature of sense, and the less rigorous Deleuze who worked with Guattari
   to trace all sense back to bodies. Žižek argues that the first Deleuze is
   actually the *true* materialism; a proper materialism accounts for the ways
   in which matter produces a spiritual double. Where I disagree with Žižek
   is in his division of Deleuze into two incommensurable theories, for his
   work with Guattari always maintained the reality of the virtual and the
   ways in which all life – not just the life of the speaking subject – was
   actual and virtual. See Slavoj Žižek, *Organs Without Bodies: Deleuze and
   Consequences*, London: Routledge, 2004.
5 TP 154–55.
6 LS 7.
7 Jacques Derrida, 'The Purveyor of Truth', in John P. Muller, and William
   J. Richardson (eds), *The Purloined Poe: Lacan, Derrida and Psychoanalytic Reading*, Baltimore, MA: Johns Hopkins University Press, 1988,
   pp. 173–212.

8 Jacques Lacan, 'Seminar on *The Purloined Letter*', in John P. Muller and William J. Richardson (eds), *The Purloined Poe: Lacan, Derrida and Psychoanalytic Reading*, Baltimore, MA: Johns Hopkins University Press, 1988.

9 And it is this style of reading that continues today in Slavoj Žižek's use of Lacan, where aspects of a film, story or cultural phenomena are read as exemplifying the relations between the 'master signifier' or the *'objet petit a'* (the object that appears as a fragment or part of a deferred fuller enjoyment or *jouissance*.

10 AO 23.

11 Jacques Derrida, *Of Grammatology*, trans. Gayatri Chakravorty Spivak, Baltimore, MA: Johns Hopkins University Press, 1976.

12 Jacques Derrida, *Dissemination*, trans. Barbara Johnson, Chicago: University of Chicago Press, 1981, p. 206.

13 TP 117.

14 Félix Guattari, *Chaosmosis: An Ethico-aesthetic Paradigm*, trans. Paul Bains and Julian Pefanis, Bloomington: Indiana University Press, 1995. Gary Genosko, *Félix Guattari: An Aberrant Introduction*, London: Continuum, 2002.

15 AO 222–40.

16 TP 460–73.

17 TP 388.

18 TP 88.

19 TP 41.

20 Foucault, *Order of Things*, p. 128.

21 Michael Hardt and Antonio Negri, *Empire*, Cambridge, MA: Harvard University Press, 2000.

22 On synthesis in its philosophical sense, see James Williams, *Gilles Deleuze's Difference and Repetition: A Critical Introduction and Guide*, Edinburgh: Edinburgh University Press, 2003, pp. 86–106.

23 AO 26.

24 AO 160.

25 Monique Wittig, *The Straight Mind and Other Essays*, Foreword by Louize Turcotte, Boston: Beacon Press, 1992.

26 TP 277.

27 AO 96–7.

28 For a reading of Freud's *Three Essays* that brings out the essential perverse nature of the sexual and its difference from self-preservative life, see Jean Laplanche, *Life and Death in Psychoanalysis*, trans. Jeffrey Mehlman, Baltimore, MA: Johns Hopkins University Press, 1976.

29 Jean-Joseph Goux, *Symbolic Economies: After Marx and Freud*, trans. Jennifer Curtiss Gage, Ithaca, NY: Cornell University Press, 1990.

30 AO 194.

31 TP 256.

32 DR 304.

33 TP 375–6.

34 LB 35.

35 ES 32.

36 S 131.
37 B 108.
38 KCP 75.
39 TP 165.
40 TP 228.
41 TP 178.
42 NP 74, 103–4.
43 TP 213.
44 TP 41.
45 Friedrich Nietzsche, *On the Genealogy of Morality*, trans. C. Diethe, Cambridge, UK: Cambridge University Press.
46 KCP 52.
47 KCP 51.
48 Christine Korsgaard, *Creating the Kingdom of Ends*, Cambridge, UK: Cambridge University Press, 1996.
49 John Rawls, 'Kantian Constructivism in Moral Theory', *John Rawls: Collected Papers*, Cambridge, MA: Harvard University Press, 1999.
50 DR 173.

CONCLUSION

1 Niall Lucy, *Debating Derrida*, Melbourne: Melbourne University Press, 1995. Christopher Norris, *Deconstruction: Theory and Practice*, 3rd edn, London: Routledge, 2002.
2 This is not to deny the significant body of Deleuze criticism that goes back to the emergence of Deleuze's own writings by his French contemporaries, nor to diminish the importance of some crucial early studies of Deleuze and Guattari before their names became widely circulated by non-specialists. Rosi Braidotti was one of the first feminist theorists to insist on the importance of Deleuze for feminist theories of sexual difference, while Elizabeth Grosz's work on the body has always challenged the linguistic paradigm, partly through reference to Deleuze. See Rosi Braidotti, *Patterns of Dissonance: A Study of Women in Contemporary Philosophy*, trans. Elizabeth Guild, Cambridge: Polity, 1990. Elizabeth Grosz, *Volatile Bodies*, Sydney: Allen and Unwin, 1994. Early lucid introductions to the thought of Deleuze include Philip Goodchild's *Deleuze and Guattari: An Introduction to the Politics of Desire*, London: Sage, 1996; Charles J. Stivale's *The Two-fold Thought of Deleuze and Guattari: Intersections and Animations*, New York: Guilford Press, 1998; and Ronald Bogue's *Deleuze and Guattari*, London: Routledge, 1989.
3 AO 329.
4 Andy Clark, *Natural-born Cyborgs: Minds, Technologies, and the Future of Human Intelligence*, Oxford: Oxford University Press, 2003.
5 Antonio Damasio, *The Feeling of What Happens: Body, Emotion and the Making of Consciousness*, New York: Vintage, 2000, p. 137.
6 V. S. Ramachandran, *The Emerging Mind*, London: Profile Books, 2003.

7 LB 67.
8 Goodchild, *Deleuze and Guattari*, p. 206.
9 PS 111.
10 WP 154.
11 TP 503.

BIBLIOGRAPHY

Ansell Pearson, Keith (1999), *Germinal Life: The Difference and Repetition of Deleuze*, London: Routledge.

Ansell Pearson, Keith (2002), *Philosophy and the Adventure of the Virtual: Bergson and the Time of Life*, London: Routledge.

Badiou, Alain (2000), *Deleuze: The Clamor of Being*, Louise Burchill (trans.), Minneapolis: University of Minnesota Press.

Bennett, David (1985), 'Parody, Postmodernism and the Politics of Reading', *Critical Quarterly*, 27:4 (Winter), 27–43.

Bennett, David (1999), 'Burghers, Burglars and Masturbators: The Sovereign Spender in the Age of Consumerism', *New Literary History*, 30:2 (Spring), 269–94.

Bergson, Henri (1911), *Creative Evolution*, Arthur Mitchell (trans.), New York: Henry Holt.

Bergson, Henri (1956), *Duration and Simultaneity*, L. Jacobson (trans.), Indianapolis: Bobbs-Merrill.

Bergson, Henri (1963), *The Two Sources of Morality and Religion*, R. Ashley Audra and C. Brereton (trans.), Indiana: University of Notre Dame Press.

Bergson, Henri (1965), *The Creative Mind*, M. L. Andison (trans.), Totowa, NJ: Littlefield, Adams and Company.

Bogue, Ronald (1989), *Deleuze and Guattari*, London: Routledge.

Bogue, Ronald (2003), *Deleuze on Cinema*, London: Routledge.

Bogue, Ronald (2003), *Deleuze on Literature*, London: Routledge.

Bogue, Ronald (2003), *Deleuze on Music, Painting and the Arts*, London: Routledge.

Bonta, Mark and John Protevi (2004), *Deleuze and Geophilosophy: A Guide and Glossary*, Edinburgh: Edinburgh University Press.

Bourdieu, Pierre (1984), *Distinction: A Social Critique of the Judgement of Taste*, Richard Nice (trans.), London: Routledge & Kegan Paul.

Braidotti, Rosi (1990), *Patterns of Dissonance: A Study of Women in Contemporary Philosophy*, Elizabeth Guild (trans.), Cambridge: Polity.

Braidotti, Rosi (2002), *Metamorphoses: Towards a Materialist Theory of Becoming*, Cambridge: Polity.

Buchanan, Ian (2000), *Deleuzism: A Metacommentary*, Edinburgh: Edinburgh University Press.

Butler, Judith (1997), *The Psychic Life of Power: Theories in Subjection*, Stanford, CA: Stanford University Press.

Carey, John, (1992), *The Intellectuals and the Masses: Pride and Prejudice among the Literary Intelligentsia, 1880–1939*, London: Faber.

Clark, Andy (2003), *Natural Born Cyborgs: Minds, Technologies, and the Future of Human Intelligence*, Oxford: Oxford University Press.

Copjec, Joan (1994), *Read My Desire: Lacan Against the Historicists*, Cambridge, MA: MIT Press.

Damasio, Antonio (2000), *The Feeling of What Happens: Body, Emotion and the Making of Consciousness*, New York: Vintage.

DeLanda, Manuel (2002), *Intensive Science and Virtual Philosophy*, London: Continuum.

Deleuze, Gilles (1983), *Nietzsche and Philosophy*, Hugh Tomlinson (trans.), London: Athlone.

Deleuze, Gilles (1984), *Kant's Critical Philosophy: The Doctrine of the Faculties*, Hugh Tomlinson and Barbara Habberjam (trans.), London: Athlone.

Deleuze, Gilles (1986), *Cinema 1: The Movement-Image*, Hugh Tomlinson and Barbara Habberjam (trans.), Minneapolis: University of Minnesota Press.

Deleuze, Gilles (1988), *Foucault*, Sean Hand (trans.), London: Athlone Press.

Deleuze, Gilles (1988), *Bergsonism*, Constantin Boundas (trans.), New York: Zone.

Deleuze, Gilles (1989), *Cinema 2: The Time-Image*, Hugh Tomlinson and Robert Galeta (trans.), Minneapolis: University of Minnesota Press.

Deleuze, Gilles (1990), *The Logic of Sense*, Mark Lester (trans.), Constantin V. Boundas (ed.), New York: Columbia University Press.

Deleuze, Gilles (1991), *Empiricism and Subjectivity: An Essay on Hume's Theory of Human Nature*, Constantin V. Boundas (trans.), New York: Columbia University Press.

Deleuze, Gilles (1992), *Expressionism in Philosophy*, Martin Joughin (trans.), New York: Zone Books.

Deleuze, Gilles (1993), *The Fold: Leibniz and the Baroque*, Tom Conley (trans.), London: Athlone.

Deleuze, Gilles (1994), *Difference and Repetition*, Paul Patton (trans.), New York: Columbia University Press.

Deleuze, Gilles (1997), *Essays: Critical and Clinical*, Daniel W. Smith and Micheal Greco (trans.), Minneapolis: University of Minnesota Press.

Deleuze, Gilles (2000), *Proust and Signs*, Richard Howard (trans.), London: Athlone.

Deleuze, Gilles (2003), *Francis Bacon: The Logic of Sensation*, Daniel Smith (trans.), London: Continuum.

Deleuze, Gilles and Félix Guattari (1983), *Anti-Oedipus: Capitalism and Schizophrenia*, Robert Hurley, Mark Seem and Helen R. Lane (trans.), Minneapolis: University of Minnesota Press.

Deleuze, Gilles and Félix Guattari (1986), *Kafka: Toward a Minor Literature*, Dana Polan (trans.), Minneapolis: University of Minnesota Press.

Deleuze, Gilles and Félix Guattari (1987), *A Thousand Plateaus: Capitalism and Schizophrenia*, Brian Massumi (trans.), Minneapolis: University of Minnesota Press.

Deleuze, Gilles and Félix Guattari (1994), *What is Philosophy?*, Hugh Tomlinson and Graham Burchill (trans.), London: Verso.

Derrida, Jacques (1981), *Dissemination*, Barbara Johnson (trans.), Chicago: University of Chicago Press.

Derrida, Jacques (1982), *Margins of Philosophy*, Alan Bass (trans.), Chicago: University of Chicago Press.

Derrida, Jacques (1988), *Limited Inc*, Gerald Graff (ed.), Evanston: Northwestern University Press.

Derrida, Jacques (1988), 'The Purveyor of Truth', in John P. Muller and William J. Richardson (eds), *The Purloined Poe: Lacan, Derrida and Psychoanalytic Reading*, Baltimore, MA: Johns Hopkins University Press, pp. 173–212.

Derrida, Jacques (1989), *Edmund Husserl's Origin of Geometry: An Introduction*, John P. Leavey (trans.), Lincoln: University of Nebraska Press.

Derrida, Jacques (1993), *Raising the Tone of Philosophy: Late Essays by Immanuel Kant – Transformative Critique by Jacques Derrida*, Peter Fenves (ed.), Baltimore, MA: Johns Hopkins University Press.

Essick, Robert N. (1980), *William Blake, Printmaker*, Princeton, NJ: Princeton University Press.

Flaxman, Gregory (2000) (ed.), *The Brain is a Screen: Deleuze and the Philosophy of Cinema*, Minneapolis: University of Minnesota Press.

Foucault, Michel (1970), *The Order of Things: An Archaeology of the Human Sciences*, London: Tavistock.

Genosko, Gary (2002), *Félix Guattari: An Aberrant Introduction*, London: Continuum.

Goldman, Jane (2003), *Modernism*, London: Palgrave.

Goodchild, Philip (1996), *Deleuze and Guattari: An Introduction to the Politics of Desire*, London: Sage.

Goux, Jean-Joseph (1990), *Symbolic Economies: After Marx and Freud*, Jennifer Curtiss Gage (trans.), Ithaca, NY: Cornell University Press.

Greer, Germaine (1970), *The Female Eunuch*, London: MacGibbon and Kee.

Grosz, Elizabeth (1994), *Volatile Bodies*, Sydney: Allen and Unwin, 1994.

Grosz, Elizabeth (2004), *In the Nick of Time*, Sydney: Allen and Unwin.

Habermas, Jürgen (1987), *Philosophical Discourse of Modernity: Twelve Lectures by Habermas*, Frederick Lawrence (trans.), Cambridge: Polity.

Hardt, Michael (1993), *Gilles Deleuze: An Apprenticeship in Philosophy*, London: UCL Press.

Hardt, Michael and Antonio Negri (2000), *Empire*, Cambridge, MA: Harvard University Press.

Hassan, Ihab (1987), *The Postmodern Turn: Essays in Postmodern Theory and Culture*, Columbus: Ohio State University Press.

Heidegger, Martin (1971), *Poetry, Language, Thought*, New York: Harper Colophon.

Heidegger, Martin (1977), *The Question Concerning Technology, and Other Essays*, William Lovitt (trans.), New York: Harper and Row.

Heidegger, Martin (1985), *What is a Thing?*, W. B. Barton and Vera Deutsch (trans.), Lanham: University Press of America.

Heidegger, Martin (1996), *Being and Time*, Joan Stambaugh (trans.), Albany, NY: State University of New York Press.

Holland, Eugene W. (1999), *Deleuze and Guattari's Anti-Oedipus: An Introduction to Schizoanalysis*, London: Routledge.

Husserl, Edmund (1970), *The Crisis of European Sciences and Transcendental Phenomenology: An Introduction to Phenomenological Philosophy*, David Carr (trans.), Evanston: Northwestern University Press.

Hutcheon, Linda (1988), *A Poetics of Postmodernism: History, Theory, Fiction*, Routledge: London.

Irigaray, Luce (1985), *Speculum of the Other Woman* (trans.), trans. Gillian C. Gill, Ithaca, NY: Cornell University Press.

Jameson, Fredric (1991), *Postmodernism, or the Cultural Logic of Late Capitalism*, London: Verso.

Kern, Stephen (1983), *The Culture of Time and Space: 1880–1918*, Cambridge, MA: Harvard University Press.

Korsgaard, Christine (1996), *Creating the Kingdom of Ends*, Cambridge, UK: Cambridge University Press.

Lacan, Jacques (1977), *Écrits*, Alan Sheridan (trans.), London: Norton.

Lambert, Gregg (2002), *The Non-Philosophy of Gilles Deleuze*, London: Continuum.

Lucy, Niall (1995), *Debating Derrida*, Melbourne: Melbourne University Press.

Lucy, Niall (1997), *Postmodern Literary Theory*, Oxford: Blackwell.

Massumi, Brian (2000), 'The Autonomy of Affect', in *Observing Complexity: Systems Theory and Postmodernism*, Dans William Rasch and Cary Wolfe (eds), Minneapolis: University of Minnesota Press, pp. 273–97.

Moran, D. (2000), *Introduction to Phenomenology*, London: Routledge.

Nietzsche, Friedrich (1997), *Untimely Meditations*, Richard J. Hollingdale (trans.), Cambridge, UK: Cambridge University Press.

Nietzsche, Friedrich (1994), *On the Genealogy of Morality*, C. Diethe (trans.), Cambridge, UK: Cambridge University Press.

Norris, Christopher (2002), *Deconstruction: Theory and Practice*, 3rd edn, London: Routledge.

Patton, Paul (2000), *Deleuze and the Political*, London: Routledge.

Pessoa, L., E. Thomson and A. Noe (1998), 'Finding Out about Filling In: A Guide to Perceptual Completion for Visual Science and the Philosophy of Perception', *Behavioural and Brain Sciences*, 21, 723–48.

Protevi, John (2001), *Political Physics: Deleuze, Derrida, and the Body Politic*, New Brunswick, NJ: Athlone Press.

Rodowick, David (1997), *Gilles Deleuze's Time Machine*, Durham, NC: Duke University Press.

Sim, Stuart (1992), *Beyond Aesthetics: Confrontations with Poststructuralism and Postmodernism*, Toronto: University of Toronto Press.

Stivale, Charles J. (1998), *The Two-fold Thought of Deleuze and Guattari: Intersections and Animations*, New York: Guilford Press.

Urmson, J. O. (1990), *The Greek Philosophical Vocabulary*, London: Duckworth.

Williams, James (2003), *Gilles Deleuze's Difference and Repetition: A Critical Introduction and Guide*, Edinburgh: Edinburgh University Press.

Wittig, Monique (1992), *The Straight Mind and Other Essays*, Louise Turcotte (Foreword), Boston: Beacon Press.

Žižek, Slavoj (ed.) (1992), *Everything You Wanted to Know About Lacan: (But were Afraid to Ask Hitchcock)*, London: Verso.

Žižek, Slavoj (2004), *Organs Without Bodies: Deleuze and Consequences*, London: Routledge.

INDEX